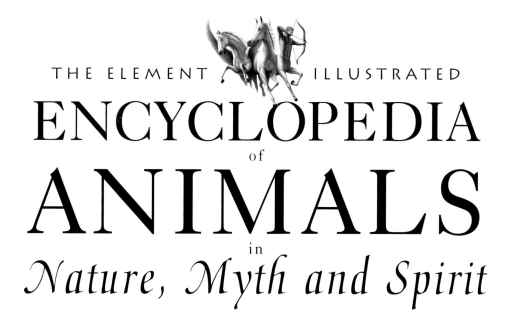

THE ELEMENT ILLUSTRATED

ENCYCLOPEDIA

of

ANIMALS

in

Nature, Myth and Spirit

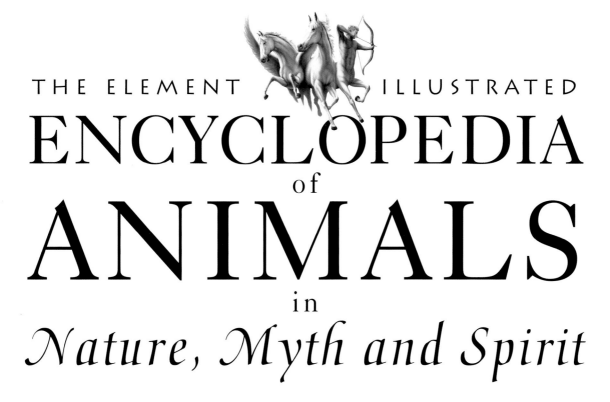

THE ELEMENT ILLUSTRATED
ENCYCLOPEDIA
of
ANIMALS
in
Nature, Myth and Spirit

Fran Pickering

ELEMENT
CHILDREN'S BOOKS

SHAFTESBURY, DORSET • BOSTON, MASSACHUSETTS • MELBOURNE, VICTORIA

*For the poet who showed
me the music of man
and the song of the stars and
because he loves animals.*

© ELEMENT CHILDREN'S BOOKS 1999
Original text © Fran Pickering 1999

First published in Great Britain in 1999
by ELEMENT CHILDREN'S BOOKS,
The Old School House, Bell Street,
Shaftesbury, Dorset SP7 8BP

Published in the U.S.A. in 1999
by ELEMENT BOOKS INC.,
160 North Washington Street
Boston MA 02114

Published in Australia in 1999 by
ELEMENT BOOKS and distributed by
Penguin Books Australia Limited,
487 Maroondah Highway,
Ringwood, Victoria 3134

Designed and created for ELEMENT BOOKS by
Bampton-Betts

ELEMENT BOOKS LIMITED
Managing Director/Publisher *Barry Cunningham*
Production Manager *Susan Sutterby*
Production Controller *Claire Legg*

BAMPTON-BETTS
Managing Editor *Claire Bampton*
Managing Art Editor *Lesley Betts*
Editorial Assistance *Janine Amos*

Reproduction by Renaissance, U.K.
Printed and bound in Singapore by Tien Wah Press

British Library Cataloguing in
Publication data available

Library of Congress Cataloguing in
Publication data available

ISBN 1-901881-84-9

Publisher's note:
This book uses American English
spelling and punctuation.

Contents

Introduction

DESPITE OUR LONG history on the planet we are only just beginning to understand the animals that share it with us. We are realizing that, like us, they are intelligent and, in many cases, just as emotional. People have always felt that we are also linked in spirit to the animal kingdom. Our animal myths and legends show this to be true.

Already animals have given us a great deal—we eat their flesh and eggs, drink their milk, and use their fur, wool, and skin to clothe our bodies. For centuries animals have been pulling our wagons, carrying our loads, giving their lives in our medical experiments, and many have become our true friends and companions.

Our myths and legends are peopled with animals that have human characteristics and reactions, perhaps because the ancient myth-makers noticed that animals have a deeper understanding that we choose to ignore.

I believe that under our shapes and skins, we all have a spirit, and the element that links us and is the magic key to understanding another creature, is love. Love is an energy, like electricity, an energy that you can use to change the way you look at things and what you do. Many people who work closely with wild animals will tell you that the emotion that provokes the best response in them is love.

This book celebrates creatures that live on the Earth in all their diversity. It is a book about animals in nature, myth and spirit.

"So we will consider your offer to buy our land. If we decide to accept, I will make one condition: that the white man must treat the beasts of this land as his brothers. I am a savage and do not understand any other way. I have seen a thousand rotting buffalos on the prairie, left by the white man who shot them from a passing train. I am a savage and do not understand how the smoking iron horse can be more important than the buffalo that we kill only to stay alive. What is man without the beasts? If all the beasts were gone men would die from a great loneliness of spirit. For whatever happens to the beasts, soon happens to man. All things are connected."

Chief Seathl

The Chief's testament was an address given to the gathering of the tribes at the time when the first governor of the new Washington territory in the U.S. was taking away the land that belonged to the Native Americans.

Fran Pickering

About this book

This page explains how the encyclopedia works. The book is divided into four sections—Earth, Air, Water, and Myth. The first three sections look at a wide variety of animals, from snakes and elephants, to whales and eagles. The last section introduces creatures from our imaginations—the creatures of myth and magic.

Between each of the sections you will find the special feature pages. These are interest pages that explore different aspects of animals in either nature, myth, or spirit. But first, read the two introduction pages at the front of the book. They take a look at the magnificent world in which we all live.

Feature page

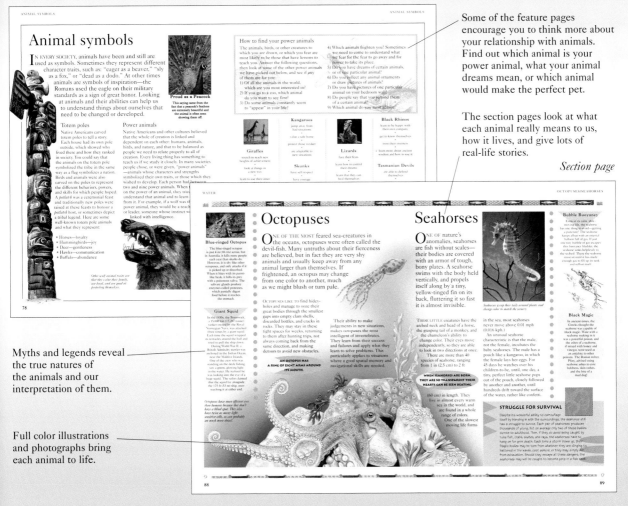

Some of the feature pages encourage you to think more about your relationship with animals. Find out which animal is your power animal, what your animal dreams mean, or which animal would make the perfect pet.

The section pages look at what each animal really means to us, how it lives, and give lots of real-life stories.

Section page

Myths and legends reveal the true natures of the animals and our interpretation of them.

Full color illustrations and photographs bring each animal to life.

A new look at animals

This encyclopedia takes a different look at animals. It allows us to explore how, as humans, we live alongside animals. It looks at the animals themselves, how they survive, and what makes them special. This book also challenges the way in which we treat animals and discusses theories that, although perhaps not yet scientifically proven, should not be ignored. It reminds us that the language we all speak is a common one—an inner language of the spirit.

Life on Earth

THIS IS PLANET Earth. Isn't it beautiful? Earth is the only planet in the solar system known to have life. Every day, we learn more and more that shows our destiny is joined to that of every other life form on the planet. We are all just a small part in something much larger, over which we have no control. Earth is like a traveling zoo, and we are linked with every other creature by our common origin and the fact that we depend on Earth and each other for our very existence.

A habitat

A habitat is the natural home of a community of plants and animals. Each habitat has its own characteristic physical and chemical features, such as climate and soil type. If something from the habitat is destroyed, its structure is weakened.

Frogs

Frogs eat mostly small invertebrates, but some will eat snails and rodents. They are the gardener's friend, eating bugs that damage plants. In turn they provide food for herons and other wading birds.

An ecosystem

An ecosystem is a distinct area in the biosphere which is made up of living things. It contains rocks, soil, the surface of the ground, and the air. Ecosystems are powered by energy from the Sun and they recycle materials such as the chemicals in plants. An ecosystem can be as large as a rain forest and desert, or as small as a drop of rainwater.

Fish

Different fish feed on different items. Some, for example, feed on plants, while others feed on small animals such as insect larvae and tadpoles.

The web of life

If you use the Internet, you will know that part of it is called the World Wide Web—a network of computers across the whole world, that are linked together in electronic communities. In a similar way, the incredible variety of life on Earth, all the plants and animals, are linked together, but in ecological, rather than electronic, communities.

Heron

The heron eats mainly fish and small amphibians. It is at the top end of the web of pond and river life, eating the frogs that eat the insects around the pond or stream.

Dragonfly

The dragonfly is among the most ancient of living creatures, having been on Earth almost 300 million years. It is the tiger of the insect world, spending its days looking for different insects to catch and eat.

All the animals in this pond depend on plants or other animals for their food.

Animals at the top of a food chain have almost no predators except, sometimes, humans.

Water snails

Water snails are scavengers. They eat the detritus, or rotting matter, at the bottom of a pond or river. In this way they help clean up the planet's waterways and recycle matter.

Toco
toucan

Earth's creatures

WE LIVE AMONGST A VAST range of different
creatures, some of them living in elements
that we cannot, such as the air and the deep
waters. Some creatures are so small it takes a
powerful microscope to see them at all, some
are so huge that if you felt one of them with
your eyes shut you could not imagine what it
looked like. The scientific term for
the whole range of life on Earth
is biodiversity.

Macaw

Caiman

Reptiles

Reptiles are vertebrates (animals with
backbones) that depend on outside
sources, such as the Sun, heated earth,
and warm stones, to keep them warm.
They breathe air and have three-
chambered hearts. Most reptiles, apart
from some snakes and lizards, lay eggs.

Coati

Amazonian
giant otters

Anaconda

Amazon
kingfisher

Invertebrates

Invertebrates are
animals without a
backbone. About 97
percent of the world's
species are invertebrates.
Invertebrates come in a great
range of body forms, from
simple sponges to
mollusks and insects.

Arapaima

Hatchet
fish

Lungfish

Fish

Fish are vertebrates that live in water and
have gills during their adult stage. Often
they have limbs in the form of fins and
propel themselves through water by
moving their body from side to side.

Discus
fish

Squirrel
monkey

Sader
monkey

Birds

Swallow-
tailed kite

Birds are vertebrates with feathers
and wings. Most of them can fly.
They are warm-blooded, have four-
chambered hearts, and their jaws are
extended into toothless beaks. Birds
have no sweat glands, so cool down
by panting, seeking shade, or flying
to a cooler location.

Chestnut
woodpecker

Giant
anteater

Tapir

Mammals

Mammals are warm-blooded
animals that have a muscular
diaphragm, hair on their bodies,
and feed their young with milk.
Some mammals have the most
highly developed nervous
system of all animals.

Four-eyed
possum

Orchid
bee

Leafcutter
ant

Agoutis

Helecon
butterfly

Common
Amazonian
frog

Scarlet
ibis

Amphibians

Amphibians are vertebrates
that can live in water and on
land. Like reptiles, their body
temperature varies with the
temperature of the environment.
Amphibians in cool regions hibernate
through winter. Their skin is
generally smooth and moist.

Rhinoceros
beetle

Giant river
turtles

Earth

· · · · · · · · · · · · · · · · · · ·

THE ELEMENT EARTH symbolizes roots and connections, wisdom and patience. Every creature that lives on planet Earth plays a large part in its development. We all live on Earth and are linked by our need to survive. The more we learn about different animal species, the more likely we are to value them and want to preserve them, and the more we will appreciate how interconnected and interdependent we all are. In this section you will read about just some of Earth's creatures—their amazing abilities and wonderful uniqueness.

SCIENTISTS BELIEVE ANIMALS FIRST MOVED FROM THE SEA TO THE LAND 400 MILLION YEARS AGO.

THERE ARE MORE THAN FOUR MILLION SPECIES ALIVE ON EARTH TODAY.

NO NEW ANIMAL HAS BEEN ADDED TO OUR DOMESTICATED LIVESTOCK FOR OVER 4,000 YEARS.

Heraldry

The lion has always been a prominent emblem in heraldry. This is probably because the nobility wanted to be associated with its image of royalty, bravery, and strength. The lion was used on shields and coats of arms in fifteen different postures, but the most popular ones are: *rampant* (as in the picture above) standing erect on its hind legs, *passant gardant* as if walking in side view, its right paw raised, *sejant*, seated, and *couchant*, lying down.

Jerome and the Lion

In A.D. 382, St Jerome became secretary to Pope Damasus. One day he was lecturing his disciples when a lion entered the school room and lifted up its paw. All the disciples left in fear, but Jerome, seeing that the paw was wounded, pulled the thorn out. The grateful lion stayed with him as a pet, which is why St Jerome is always shown accompanied by a lion.

A lioness is pregnant for three and a half months. When its cubs arrive, other lionesses help to nurse the young.

Lions

Lions live in prides of between six and 20 lions. They are the most sociable animal of the cat family.

FOR CENTURIES, THE LION has been known as the "king of the beasts." This may be because with its strength and confidence, it seems to have absolute control over everything in the animal kingdom —very few animals are able to even challenge a lion. To us, the lion symbolizes the strength, nobility, and courage we admire.

THERE ARE FIVE KINDS of lion alive today: the Asian lion, which lives in the Gir Forest Reserve in northwest India, and four types of African lion. African lions are larger and more impressive

LIONS CAN CARRY TWICE THEIR OWN WEIGHT.

than the Indian lion.

A mature African lion can stand 4 ft (1.2 m) high, measure over 10 ft (3 m) in length, and weigh an average of 400 lb (181 kg)— about three times as much as a human being.

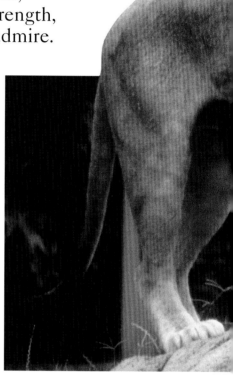

LIONS HUM WHEN HAPPY, AND COUGH TO WARN SOMEONE OFF!

The stockier Asian lion has a smaller mane, a thicker coat with hairy elbows, and a longer tail tassel.

Although lions may sit alone for hours, staring in regal aloofness into the distance, or dozing idly for 18–20 hours a day, they are not solitary by choice and need the support of a pride. In fact, they are the only members of the big

A LION'S HEART BEATS AROUND 40 TIMES A MINUTE.

A lion can run 298 ft (91 m) in just four seconds, and can bring down most prey on its own. However, it relies hugely on the lionesses. These females are marvellous examples of feline power. The lioness does most of the hunting to feed the pride, sometimes working on her own if the prey is small, such as a wart hog, or in a team with other lionesses when chasing buffalo or zebra. She is more active than the male and is more alert at all times. The

A LION'S ROAR CAN BE HEARD 5 MILES (8 KM) AWAY.

lioness is the real heart of the pride. The males may only last three years or so before younger males come to challenge them and take their place, but the females stay in the group.

Just like all cats, a lion has an intense, unblinking stare, a stare that really *sees* what it is looking at and reminds you that it is one of the most efficient natural killing machines on the planet.

cat family to live in groups. Male lions form partnerships with other males, to breed with and defend a pride of female lions. Usually these partnerships are with brothers or cousins reared in the same group. Between four and nine close male relatives may join forces. A solitary male will never join with more than one or two other males if they are all non-relatives. This ensures that most of the cubs born to the pride belong to the same family, keeping the genetic line strong.

The Big Yawn

That lazy yawn of a sprawling lion may not be so harmless as it seems. The yawn accelerates the flow of blood through the lion's body, toning up its muscles, and making available an instant supply of energy that is needed by any lion that is just about to strike!

Lion Dances

In China, the New Year is celebrated with a lion dance to bring good luck. Five or more dancers make up the lion procession. One wears the mask head, one the body, and the other three are musicians: a drummer, a gong player, and a cymbalist. Lion colors have meanings: a black lion is a fighting lion, a red lion is full of happiness and prosperity, and a multicolored lion is the oldest and wisest.

Tiger Talk

A tiger has quite a range of sounds. It coughs to frighten animals away from a kill, moans in displeasure, barks to call to another tiger, hisses to blow insects from a kill, and roars in anger. One tiger seen stalking a wild buffalo, was even heard to make a noise like a bull's bellow, perhaps to fool the buffalo into coming nearer!

The Java Sarong

Many years ago, on the island of Java, lived a magician who owned little pieces from a magic sarong. The material was yellow with black stripes and just big enough to wrap around his big toe. Once on the toe, the sarong stretched to cover the magician completely. As soon as this happened, he changed into a tiger, ready to go out and prowl through the forest.

Tigers

WILLIAM BLAKE, in his poem about tigers, described the animal as "burning bright in the forest of the night." Tigers are the biggest and most magnificent of all the cats. They embody grace, beauty, and power, but are deadly killing machines. From the age of two years old, they live and hunt alone, masters of silent stalking and sudden ambush.

WHEN A TIGER IS IN its natural habitat, its black and orange markings match the patterns made by the Sun's rays or moonlight on grass and trees. It can creep silently, from bush to bush or through the long grass, without being seen, until close enough to leap on its prey. A tiger is at the top of its food chain—it eats almost anything, but nothing eats it. It prefers to eat hoofed animals, although it has been

THE INDIAN NAME FOR A TIGER IS "SHER."

known to catch birds, fish, crocodiles, and even bears.

A tiger often attacks its prey from the side or behind. Once within leaping range, a tiger breaks cover and jumps onto the back of the animal. It then wraps its paws around the animal's throat, before plunging its long

teeth into the animal's neck, more often than not snapping the creature's spine. If the prey is not then dead, one bite to the throat finishes the job.

After a kill the tiger drags the animal's body out of sight and eats it. A tiger can devour up to 66 lb (30 kg) of meat at one time, and once it has eaten its fill, covers the remains of the prey with leaves, returning to the carcase each night until it is finished.

A tiger ambushes prey that

comes to rivers to drink. It also enjoys lounging in water. However, at this time it is most vulnerable, so it often walks backward into water, keeping a careful lookout at the same time.

At the beginning of this century, there were eight varieties of tiger, now there are only five and probably little more than 5,000 tigers left on the planet. Of these, the Siberian tiger is the largest and one of the most endangered. From nose to tail, a Siberian tiger can measure between

10–13 ft (3–4 m) and weigh, on average, up to 500 lb (227 kg.) The heaviest recorded was a male weighing 847 lb (384 kg.) Only 20–30 South China tigers remain and these are in wildlife reserves or zoos. It is a desperate sight to

All tiger cubs stay with their mother until they are two years old, although some may stay until they are about five years old.

MAN-EATING TIGERS

Tigers usually have to be desperately hungry to eat people, but some have been known to get a taste for human flesh and become man-eaters. The man-eating record is held by a tigress in Nepal in the early 1900s, who is supposed to have eaten 438 people in just eight years. One tigress killed 127 people in the province of Scindia, in India, frightening people from the main roads for months. In a single year, when records were kept in India, tigers killed 22,000 people and 80,000 domestic cattle. Some tiger experts claim that tigers only become man-eaters when wounded or crippled, or if they are a starving female with young to feed.

see a caged tiger that cannot use its power or employ its natural camouflage, but then again, perhaps it is better to see this magnificent cat caged, than never to see it again?

A tiger creeping through the long grass is almost invisible.

Thai Tigers

A Thai myth tells that long ago, in the dense forest that once covered Thailand, there lived a huge animal with the body of an elephant and the head of a tiger. King Phan of Nakhon Pathom City ordered three brave hunters to catch the strange animal. When it was in captivity, the king bred a new race of war elephants. Villagers in Thailand still celebrate this myth once a year by making models of the tiger-headed elephant.

Bear Constellation

The bear has stirred people's imagination so much it has been given a place in the stars: Ursa Major—the Great Bear, and Ursa Minor—the Little Bear. One of the Greek myths tells the story of how the god Zeus fell in love with the nymph Callisto, and had a son called Arcas. His wife, the goddess Hera, was so jealous that she changed Callisto into a bear. To protect Callisto and Arcas from any further wrath, Zeus put them both into the sky as star constellations.

Medicine Woman

A Native American tale tells the story of the Bear Medicine Woman. While she was still in the womb, her father killed a bear. The spirit of the bear entered her body and she grew up to become the Bear Medicine Woman. The Bear Medicine ceremony is still celebrated in some parts of America, where people call for healing powers by imitating the actions of a bear.

Bears love the taste of fish and go into rivers during the summer to catch salmon as the fish head upstream.

Bears

IN ANCIENT LEGENDS, bears have been considered kin to humans. This may be because, like us, they can stand and walk on two legs. Bears are incredibly strong. In fact, no animal of equal size is more powerful. Despite their great size and strength, bears are usually gentle and good-natured and do not often seek out trouble. However, they have quick tempers, and if annoyed their mood can change from playful to angry with little warning.

THERE ARE NINE different types of bear and they can be found in all parts of the world except Australia, Africa, and Antarctica. The largest bear is the Alaskan brown bear, which stands 10–11 ft (3–3.4 m) high, and the smallest is the sun bear, which lives in Southern Asia. It is only about 4 ft (1.2 m) tall.

Bears eat berries, nuts, roots, insects, fish, and any small animals they happen to catch.

BEARS SLAP THE GROUND AND WOOF WHEN THEY ARE ABOUT TO ATTACK.

FIVE SPECIES OF BEAR ARE ON THE ENDANGERED ANIMAL LIST.

Their special skill is fishing, where they stand in rapids and hook out fish with their long, sharp claws. Bears also love honey, and often raid wild or cultivated bee hives. They rarely forget where they have found food and will travel up to 60 miles (97 km) to a past site.

Female bears are wonderful mothers and keep their young with them for two to seven years, training them well. The females provide food for their cubs, as bear cubs do not fish on their own until they are around two years old. For these first years, they sit on the bank and watch their mother at work, learning the tricks of her trade. She-bears are very protective of their young and even the largest of the males tend

**BLACK BEARS CAN RUN
AS FAST AS SOME HORSES.**

to avoid females with cubs, even
though they are likely to weigh
twice as much as them.

All bears are astonishingly swift.
The black bear can reach running
speeds of 35–40 mph (56–64 kph)
over short distances, which makes
them fierce predators.

Probably the most well-known
bear is the grizzly, named for its
"grizzled" coat, not because it

BRIGHT BEAR

In 1993, a Russian tourist agent was asked
to take some American visitors on a wild bear hunt.
Desperate to please his clients, the agent bought a bear
from a Russian circus and released it into Moscow's Perdelkino
Forest. The bear, not used to being loose, wandered around
aimlessly while the American party closed in on him, ready
to shoot. Meanwhile, a postman cycling through the forest
bumped into the bear. Surprised and a little bit scared, he fell
off his bike and ran off. The bear, remembering his days in the
circus, picked up the bicycle and cycled off to safety, leaving
the American tourists wandering around the forest for hours!

moans a lot! The grizzly bear can
be any color from honey to almost
black, but its hairs are tipped
with white or silver.

Some bears, such as the Asian
and American black bears,
conserve energy by hibernating.
At the first sign of winter,
when food becomes scarce,
they find themselves a cave,
tree, or deep pile of leaves
and drift off into a deep
sleep until spring.

Forest Rescue

In 1997, a three-year-old girl
became lost in a forest in the
U.S. After three days and two
nights, expecting the little girl
to have died of hypothermia, a
search party found her asleep
under a tree. The girl claimed
that while lost she had met a
bear with two cubs. She spent
the day playing with the cubs,
and when night fell, the she-
bear licked the cubs and the
girl. Then all four curled up
together and fell asleep.

Dancing Bears

In parts of Asia and Europe,
bears are made to dance on the
streets to entertain tourists.
Wild baby bears are taken from
their mothers, forced to stand
upright, and taught to "dance"
on hot metal trays that burn
their feet. A dancing bear is
controlled by the pain caused
when a chain pulls on a ring
inserted through the palate
between its mouth and nostrils.

*The bear makes a grim enemy
when reared up on its hind
legs in an aggressive stance, but it
is playful too, and can sometimes
be seen whizzing down snow-
covered slopes in winter.*

White Elephant

The term "white elephant" is used to refer to something costly, but useless. In Thailand all the white elephants belong to the king by law. Stories tell of kings who gave a white elephant to courtiers they wished to ruin. The elephant required expensive attention but, being royal, could not be put to work to earn its keep!

Elephant Graveyards

Do elephants go to a special place to die? No, they don't! However, they do go off *alone* to die. They also take an interest in elephant bones. One young elephant, on finding the jaw bone of its dead mother, spent a day fondling it. Elephants have been seen covering their dead with leaves and branches.

Elephants often entwine trunks and clash their ivory tusks together in play.

Elephants

ALTHOUGH THESE magnificent animals are still wild, they have been used by humans as beasts of burden for thousands of years. Carved seals, 5,000 years old, from the Indus Valley, show elephants with rugs over them and we know that Hannibal, the famous general, took 38 elephants with his army across the Alps in 218 B.C. Even today, elephants are decorated for and ridden in festivals, and used to carry heavy loads across land.

ONCE ELEPHANTS lived in most parts of the world, but as humans cultivated the land, the areas in which elephants could roam became fewer and fewer.

Today the only elephants are found in India and Africa, and even those are threatened with extinction. They are hunted for their ivory tusks, so most of them that survive live in protected parks and reserves.

Elephants spend between 18 and 20 hours a day eating up to 550 lb (250 kg) of vegetation. They use their long trunks to suck up around 26 gallons (100 liters) a day. Each trunk full holds around 1.2 gallons (4.5 liters.)

People who work closely with animals believe that elephants have strong emotional ties to one another. They are highly intelligent and sensitive creatures, and contact

Hindu temples in India have stables of elephants. The animals are decorated and ridden in ceremonial processions.

ELEPHANTS SOMETIMES PLAY FOOTBALL WITH BALLS OF EARTH.

the ear of its human foster mother.

Elephants sometimes look as if they are crying as their eyes water heavily at times, often in situations that would make us sad, such as being captured, injured, scolded, separated from their families, or when a close friend dies. One photograph shows a young circus elephant with tears rolling down its cheeks as it stands with chains cutting deep into its ankles.

Elephants can show compassion, supporting sick or injured members of their group by propping them up on either side

ELEPHANTS PURR IF THEY LOSE SIGHT OF EACH OTHER IN THE WILD.

and slowing down the group's pace so that they all stay together. One female elephant in Murchison Falls National Park, U.S., carried her dead calf around for three days, scraped a shallow grave under a tree, buried the calf, and stood guard for a few more days, eating nothing until finally she left the site.

ELEPHANTS ARE THE LARGEST LIVING LAND MAMMALS ON EARTH.

with family members and other elephants is extremely important to them. Elephant babies like to touch their mother whilst they feed—one baby elephant in an elephant orphanage in Kenya would only drink from its bottle if it could stick its trunk into

Ganesha

Ganesha is the Hindu god of wisdom and good luck, the "Remover of Obstacles," whose power is called upon at the start of a journey or important task. An elephant-headed god who rides on the back of a rat, he is sometimes shown sitting on a lotus surrounded by a ring of skulls. Statues of this god are found mainly in India, but also on the island of Java and in Bali.

Indian or African?

The most obvious difference between African and Indian elephants is size. The African elephant is about 11 ft (3.4 m) tall at the shoulder and has much larger ears than the Indian elephant. The Indian elephant, grows to 10 ft (3 m) at its tallest point —the arch of the back, which is slightly humped.

ELEPHANT ARTISTS

Tildy, an elephant at New York Zoo, U.S., was seen scratching drawings in the dust with a stick. Its keeper gave it pots of paints and a long brush, and before long it had created enough paintings for an exhibition. In 1980, the keeper of Siri, a young Indian elephant, gave it a pencil and a drawing pad and it began to draw with enthusiasm. Samples of the work were sent to artists, and one comment was that they showed "flair, decisiveness, and originality." Many captive elephants use sticks or stones to draw. In fact, Carol, an Indian elephant at San Diego Zoo, U.S., paints with colors, as does Ruby, an Asian elephant who lives in Phoenix, Arizona, U.S.

WWF

The giant panda is used as the logo for WWF (World Wide Fund For Nature.) WWF chose the panda as it is the best-known and -loved of all the endangered species. WWF began work on panda conservation in China in 1980 and today has spent close to $11 million there. WWF has worked with the Chinese government to establish 14 new reserves, covering a total of 3,000 square miles (7,800 km²) of their 7,000 square mile(18,100 km²) habitat will be protected forever.

Panda's Stare

Many animals are instinctively afraid of two large eyes staring directly at them, as in the wild it can be taken as a sign of attack. The panda's huge black circles around its eyes exaggerate this stare especially as at a distance, its ears can look like two more eyes, doubling its threatening power!

Giant pandas

ALTHOUGH THEY HAVE been living on Earth for millions of years and were once the pets of Chinese emperors, giant pandas are now extremely rare, endangered animals that live wild in six small mountainous forest areas of China. Solitary animals that spend most of their time alone, in the wild, they are exceedingly shy of humans. They are, however, one of the most popular and best-loved animals.

THE GIANT PANDA STANDS between 4–5 ft (1.2–1.5 m) tall, has a 5 in (12.5 cm) tail, and weighs an average of 176–221 lb (80–100 kg.) The giant panda is very furry— even the soles of its feet are covered in hair. The black and white fur is not soft and silky as it looks from a distance, but hard, coarse, and thick.

Pandas are carnivores that have

adapted well to their environment and have mainly a vegetarian diet. They eat fish and rodents, but 99 percent of what they eat is made up of the stem, shoots, and leaves of the bamboo plant. Pandas have an elongated wrist bone that acts rather like our thumb, allowing them to hold the bamboo stalks while they chew on them.

UNLIKE OTHER BEARS, GIANT PANDAS DO NOT HIBERNATE.

Large areas of bamboo forests are being cleared regularly, making life harder and harder for the giant panda.

TINY PANDA BABIES WEIGH AS LITTLE AS 3 OZ (100 G) AT BIRTH.

Hidden in the forest, the panda spends most of its time eating. In fact, it gets through about 33 lb (15 kg) of bamboo in only 14 hours—that's about 10 percent of its body weight. A panda only digests a small amount of its food, and bamboo is very poor in nutrients, so this is probably why it eats such a lot and so fast.

JOYFUL PANDA

Most of the time, pandas rarely show their emotions in an obvious way. They are one of the most difficult animals to come to understand, their faces showing little of their feelings or reactions. However, one two-year old panda from a Chinese center had spent most of its life in a darkened cage. One day it was moved to an outdoor enclosure. Immediately the panda erupted into a ball of joy. It pranced up a hill in the compound and then somersaulted all the way down. It repeated this over and over again, unable to contain its pleasure at being outside and free to play in the wild.

Although the bamboo plant can take between ten and 100 years to flower, once it has produced seeds it dies. The seeds may take several years to grow into new plants. During this time, the pandas have to either change

PERE ARMAND DAVID WAS THE FIRST EUROPEAN TO DESCRIBE THE GIANT PANDA IN 1869.

their diet or move on to where the bamboo has not yet flowered just to survive.

Giant pandas are under threat because of the destruction of the bamboo forests, which leaves fewer and fewer places for them to live and eat. Today there are less than 1,000 wild pandas alive on Earth.

Magical Pandas

Until A.D. 2, the panda was considered rare and semi-divine in China. From 206 B.C. to A.D. 24, Chinese emperors kept rare beasts in the palace gardens and the most treasured of these were the pandas. The Chinese poet Bai Juyo wrote that the panda had magical powers that could ward off evil spirits and natural disasters, and prevent disease.

Black Eyes

Legends tell that a long time ago, when the panda's fur was pure white, one of its friends was the youngest girl of four sisters. They often laughed and played together happily. One day, a hungry tiger crept up on them. The tiger was about the kill the panda, when the panda's friend rushed to stop the attack and was instead killed herself. The panda was so distressed that it rubbed black ashes on its arms as a sign of mourning and cried for a long time, rubbing its eyes with his paws. From that day onward, the panda has had black rings around its eyes.

Horses

Famous Horse

Clever Hans was a famous counting horse. In front of a crowd, his trainer would ask him to perform multiplication sums such as times two by four. Hans would tap out the answer with his foot—in this case, eight. How did he do it? Hans used his naturally heightened senses to pick up on the tiny eyebrow movements of his trainer, which he made just before Hans was nearing the correct number of taps!

The horses of the Camargue, in France, live in the wild, but are used to herd cattle.

PERHAPS MORE THAN most animals, horses have been drawn into the world of humans. For centuries they have been hunted, farmed, used as pack horses, harnessed to pull carts, carriages, ploughs, and chariots, taken into wars, and used for entertainment. Humans and horses have forged many friendships, from small girls and their ponies, to Alexander the Great and his beloved horse Bucephalus.

LONG AGO, WILD HORSES were stalked by carnivorous predators such as big cats and wolves. Since these enemies were some of the fastest and stealthiest animals on the planet, horses needed excellent instincts to survive, and they developed

THERE ARE OVER 100 BREEDS OF DOMESTICATED HORSE.

one of the most sensitive alarm systems in nature. Despite centuries of association with humans, horses still retain these hair-trigger instincts.

Even in darkness, they can see movements unnoticed by most

For centuries horses have been working for people's benefit.

SOME RACE HORSES GALLOP AT MORE THAN 40 MPH (64 KPH.)

horse's fear and build up trust. Frank Bell, an American horse whisperer who studied the ways of the American Plains Indians with horses, says that when he makes contact with a new horse the most important thing is the first impression he makes on the horse, as it is the first impression that links directly to these age-old instincts. The horse looks to see if he should run away or if it is

other species, including humans, they can hear tiny sounds beyond human hearing, and can smell a carnivore at great distance. Because they are naturally fearful, any unknown or unexpected thing picked up by these senses causes a horse to react in alarm and try to follow its basic instinct to explode into flight and run for survival.

WHEN HORSES WALK, THEY MOVE THEIR DIAGONALLY OPPOSITE LEGS AT THE SAME TIME.

If a horse is treated roughly or mishandled, its basic nature can take over, and that first instinct to run from danger will be very strong. It will try to get away and so, often, will become labeled as wild or unmanageable.

ADULT HORSES HAVE BETWEEN 40 AND 42 TEETH.

Horse whisperers are trainers who work to understand these deep instincts of fear and self-protection by flight. They use gentle, calm gestures to allay a

LIFE LINE

Once a horse and a bull shared the same field on a farm. The bull was sold, and the horse soon became ill. A vet was called, but he couldn't find anything medically wrong with the horse. The only conclusion he could draw was that the horse was dying of a broken heart. The farmer called the new owner of the bull and asked him to lead the bull to his telephone receiver. The farmer then held her receiver to the horse's mouth and made it whinny. On hearing the noise, the bull pricked up his ears and bellowed loudly. The horse whinnied back, and so began the world's oddest telephone conversation! This became a daily ritual and the horse made a full recovery.

safe to stay. Using caresses and strokes to soothe the horse and unravel years of evolutionary conditioning, Bell gradually transforms the horse's instinctive distrust of humans. The horse is then willing to do anything for him because it trusts him. Bell says, "The word 'love' is not inappropriate."

Horseshoes

Most horses are fitted with metal shoes to protect their hooves on hard roads and surfaces. The first horseshoes were made of leather and called "hipposandals." Horseshoes are believed to be lucky, but only if they are hung with the opening at the top!

Comanche

Captain Keogh of the U.S. Cavalry rode a horse, called Comanche, in the Battle of Little Big Horn in 1876. Although wounded and hardly able to stand, Comanche carried his master for many hours. Comanche's heroic deed has made him one of the most famous horses in America.

At the end of the battle, Comanche was the only horse left alive.

Buffalo Dance

In southern France, cave paintings dating from around 10,000–30,000 B.C., show masked men luring buffalo toward a cliff to be killed on the rocks below by acting out a lively dance step. The Blackfoot Indians of Montana in Canada used to hunt buffalo in a similar way. Legend has it that the Blackfoot Indians learned the slow and solemn ritual dance from the buffalo after a young woman agreed to marry a bull buffalo, in exchange for the herd sacrificing themselves so the tribe could eat.

Buffalo and bison

THROUGHOUT HISTORY, buffalo and bison have been symbols of abundance and sacred life. Their meat fed people, their hides were used to make clothes and shelters, their sinews for thread, and their bones to make tools, needles, and knives. They symbolized generosity of spirit as they gave themselves entirely to the needs of humans.

THE AMERICAN BUFFALO is actually a bison. The name "buffalo" applies to those animals found in Asia and Africa. The American buffalo is an impressive animal. It has a great shaggy head and powerful, humped shoulders, both covered in a cape of brown-black

ONE WHITE BUFFALO IS BORN FOR EVERY FIVE MILLION BROWN BUFFALO.

fur. Male buffalo, called bulls, weigh in at about 1,600 lbs (725 kg,) females, called cows, slightly less at 1,000 lbs (453 kg.)

BUFFALOS ENJOY LYING IN WATER AND WALLOWING IN MUD.

They stand around 6.2 ft (1.9 m) tall at the shoulders, with a $6^1/_2$–$11^1/_2$ ft (2–3.5 m) body length. That's larger than the African buffalo, which has a body length of around $6^1/_2$–$9^1/_2$ ft (2–2.9 m.)

The African buffalo has larger, curved horns and a much smaller mane. It is the most aggressive of all the buffalos, quite capable of defeating a lion. The longest horns grown by any animal are those of the Indian buffalo. On the curve, they can measure over 13 ft (4 m) from tip to tip.

Buffalo are primarily grazers, herbivores, that feed in both the morning and the evening. They rest up during the day, chewing the cud or wallowing in water, mud, or dust to rid themselves of the parasites that live on their bodies.

Once the buffalo herds on the American plains were like brown seas, stretching from horizon to horizon. Thomas Farnham, while traveling the Santa Fe Trail, Mexico in 1839, was in the midst of a buffalo herd for three days. He estimated there were well

ONE HERD OF BUFFALO IN ZIMBABWE HAS BEEN LED BY AN ELEPHANT FOR 20 YEARS.

over a million of them covering an area about 1,350 square miles (3,496.5 km².) The vast herds were made up of smaller family groups of 50–100, and were usually led by an old female.

Buffalo Birds

Two birds stay close to a buffalo throughout the whole of its life. The cattle egret perches on its back, flying down to grab the insects disturbed by the buffalo's hooves in the grass. The oxpecker stays even closer, feeding on the ticks in the buffalo's hide. It lives almost permanently on the buffalo's back, sometimes even courting and mating there.

AWKWARD BUFFALO

Herdsman Michell Pablo made three attempts to round up some buffalo he had sold to the Canadian government. First he tried to load them into a cattle car, and led by an old bull, the group trotted into the railroad yard. Without changing pace the group trotted up the ramp into the car, smashed through the wooden rear, and carried on trotting back up the valley and away. Next they were herded into a corral against a steep, cliff wall. The group ran straight into the corral and out again—up the cliff! Finally, when a small group were successfully penned, a big bull splintered the planking with its horns and led the group to freedom.

Buffalo and bison were hunted almost to extinction. Today the bison herds in the U.S. have grown to about 35,000.

Wolves

Wolf and Crane

A small meat bone was stuck in the wolf's throat. The crane agreed to try and remove it. It stuck its long neck down the wolf's throat and pulled out the bone. When the crane asked for a reward the wolf replied: "Be content. You have put your head inside a wolf's mouth and taken it out again in safety. That ought to be reward enough for you!"

Wolves survive freezing temperatures by lying with their backs to the wind, tucking their noses between their legs, and covering their faces with their thick tails.

WOLVES ARE TRULY free spirits, yet they live in social structures with very defined rules. Within their packs, which rarely have more than 12 members, disobedience, selfishness, and unruly behavior are not tolerated. Each pack is led by a dominant pair, the alpha male and alpha female, who stay together for life. The alpha male signals its rank by carrying its tail higher than the others.

THE WHOLE PACK shows great loyalty to the alpha pair, which are treated with great affection and tolerance. Wolves show respect by folding back their ears and squeezing their tails between their legs.

If the alpha female gives birth, the pack is responsible for rearing her pups. Before the pups are born, the mother digs

WOLVES CAN TRAVEL UP TO 31-40 MILES (50–65 KM) A NIGHT.

out a den under the forest floor, sometimes helped by other females of the pack. The den is like a small cave, reached by a short tunnel. When the mother is giving birth inside the den, the pack gathers outside. As each pup is born, the wolves howl loudly, wag their tails,

Wolves howl to keep in touch with each other or to warn rival packs to keep away.

dominant animal soon prevails and the challenger shows submission, often by lying on its back with its throat exposed.

A wolf has extremely sharp hearing, and a sense of smell that is more than a thousand times more acute than a human's. Its pointed nose encourages air to circulate around the odour-sensitive cells inside. One researcher found a five-month-old cub that had picked up the smell of a porcupine in a field a mile (one and a half kilometers) away.

Pack members hunt together, co-operating to run down prey such as deer, caribou, and wild horses. They also eat small

A WOLF CAN EAT UP TO 20 LB (9 KG) OF FOOD AT ANY ONE TIME.

animals such as mice, fish, and crabs.

The two main species of wolf are the gray wolf and the smaller red wolf. The gray wolf varies in size and coat color, from all black to the white of the Arctic wolf. An adult male gray wolf averages 88 lb (40 kg) in weight and 5–6¹/₂ ft (1.5–2 m) in length.

and sniff and lick one another.

Wolf pups are carefully raised and trained. While the pack goes out to hunt, one wolf, called the aunt, stays behind with the pups.

Squabbles in a wolf pack are frequent, but controlled. The

THE MANED WOLF AND THE CRAB-EATING WOLF ARE MAINLY NOCTURNAL.

Romulus and Remus

In 8 B.C., Romulus and Remus were baby twin heirs to the throne of Latium. Their uncle ordered the babies to be killed, but a servant put them in a wooden chest on the River Tiber instead. This was washed onto the banks near the site of present-day Rome. There a she-wolf found them and brought them up until they were adopted by Faustulus, one of the royal shepherds.

Happy Eater

It is said that when the wolf eats, all eat. In winter, when wolves have eaten their fill of a kill, small mammals such as hares, weasels, porcupines, mice, and voles, come to nibble on the flesh, while birds swoop down to grab a beak-full.

LONG MEMORY

A naturalist exploring the Canadian wilderness came upon a she-wolf caught by its foot in a trap. Its pup sat beside it. The pair had obviously been there for some time, and were both very hungry. The naturalist fed the pup, and slept nearby until he felt the wolf trusted him. He then released it. The wolf then made it clear it wanted him to follow, and led him to its pack. The naturalist stayed with the pack for a few days, until the pack moved on. Some years later, the naturalist was camping in the same area, when a wolf appeared and stood gazing at him. By its scarred foot, he recognized it as the same wolf he had saved.

Fox, Ass, and Lion

The fox, ass, and lion went hunting together. After catching their prey, the ass divided the spoils into three piles. The lion roared with anger because it wanted all the food and killed the ass. The fox, wanting to stay alive, put the meat in one pile and offered it to the lion saying it was happy with the scraps. To this day the fox still eats scraps.

Many red foxes live in towns and cities. They scavenge from dustbins and rubbish tips after dark.

Foxes

THE FOLKLORE OF MANY countries sees the fox as a trickster—a magical animal able to change shape, and always having an intent to deceive. This is probably because foxes are opportunistic, adapting their behavior to different circumstances, and can creep around unseen. Foxes are infamous for their cunning and slyness, but should be admired for their alertness, intelligence, and keen observation.

THE RED FOX IS the most common of all the foxes. It is found in Canada, U.S., Europe, Australia, and much of Asia, and in nearly all habitats from mountain tops and sand dunes, to salt marshes and town centers. Each red fox family holds its own territory, which may be as small as 77 square feet (200 m²) for foxes that have adapted to town life, and as large as 25 square miles (65 km²) for

foxes in hill country.

Foxes are cautious by nature, and only come out of hiding at dusk. Most town sightings of foxes happen as they are caught in car headlights while crossing the road.

A fox's senses are keen. It is able to see movement and objects on the very edge of its field of vision. It is a master of stealth and camouflage, and makes the very best use of any available cover. Its sense of smell is also extremely highly developed.

Foxes have a wide and varied

BAT-EARED FOXES HAVE LARGE EARS. THEY HUNT THEIR PREY BY SOUND.

diet, eating mainly small mammals, earthworms, beetles, fruit, and carrion. Urban foxes steal food from dustbins, bird tables, compost heaps, and rubbish dumps. They are scavengers rather than predators.

Arctic foxes could not survive without previously buried food stores to rely on. They tend to kill everything in sight, probably responding to a need to obtain extra food for storage, even though they often cannot carry away all they have destroyed. Arctic foxes have excellent

A FOX'S TAIL IS CALLED ITS BRUSH.

memories, burying surplus food in many places and remembering each one. The icy climate keeps their supply of birds, animals, and even eggs well-preserved.

When it comes to eating, male foxes, called dogs, usually eat more than females, called vixens. However, when their cubs are born, the dog goes to great trouble to bring food for the vixen, even going without himself until she is full. The dog continues with this behavior until the cubs are able to fend for themselves in the wild, then he returns to a more independent way of life, looking only after himself.

Play is important to a fox, and both the dog-fox and vixen play with their cubs. They have at least 22 play signals and seem also to communicate inaudibly. One vixen was spotted watching from the den entrance as her three cubs played nearby. One of the cubs set off determinedly across the field to the far hedge.

Young male cubs leave the den, but young females stay, which sometimes leaves up to five vixens with one dominant dog fox.

CUNNING CREATURES

When in danger, foxes use every trick in the book to survive. One fox was seen being chased by hounds. It came to a stream, across which an old tree had fallen, ran halfway across the log, peered over the side, and spotted a tiny island of dry ground in the middle of the stream. It jumped down to this tiny island, then leapt back onto the bank it had just come from and ran off. Not long after, the hounds came to the log, sniffed the fox's scent, and ran across it to the other bank where suddenly they lost the scent. After running around in circles for some time the hounds finally gave up the chase.

Immediately the vixen rose to her feet, stood very still, and pointed her muzzle in its direction. In a few seconds, the cub slowed, turned, looked at its mother, and hurried back home.

Foxes have been and still are being treated cruelly by humankind. They are either hunted as a sport, or killed by fur trappers and rabies controllers. Worldwide, foxes are one of the most persecuted mammals.

Inari

Inari is the Japanese god of food, or goddess of rice, and is both male and female. His/her messenger is the fox and it is believed that he/she can change into a fox. In many Japanese households Inari is seen as a symbol of prosperity and friendship, and many Japanese towns have Inari shrines guarded by statues of foxes. Inari's central temple Fushimi-Inara, in south-east Kyoto city, was built around A.D. 700.

Snake Charming

A popular belief is that snakes can be charmed into a trance by flute music. In fact, this is completely untrue. Snakes have no ear membranes and are deaf to all but the lowest frequencies. It is not the sound of the snake charmer's flute that affects the snake, but the swaying movements of the man and pipe, and the vibrations of sound traveling through the ground!

Did You Know...

A Jacobson's organ is a small pouch found in the mouths of snakes and other reptiles. It is lined with special cells, which allow the snake to sense and track its prey by tasting the air, water, or ground when it flicks its tongue in and out. A snake flicks its forked tongue out every few seconds.

Serpent Staff

Adopted as the badge of the Royal Army Medical Corps, this symbol of a staff with two snakes twisted around it was the emblem of Asclepius, the Greek god of medicine. The magic wand of Hermes, the Greek messenger of the gods had silver wings and two snakes coiled round it. The Bible tells of Moses lifting up a brass snake with power to heal all those that looked on it.

Snakes

FOR CENTURIES, people around the world have been both fascinated and frightened by snakes. In eastern countries snakes are symbols of new beginnings and transformations, probably because they regularly shed their skins and emerge with new ones. In the West, in Christian countries, snakes have been seen as evil, their form taken by the devil to tempt Eve in the Garden of Eden.

THE MOST OBVIOUS thing about snakes is that they have no limbs. With no arms or legs, it seems as if they glide along by magic. In fact, snakes move by hitching their scales over rough parts of ground and then extending the

Snakes have no eyelids, their eyes are protected by clear scales.

RATTLESNAKES SHAKE THEIR TAILS TO MAKE A LOUD WHIRRING NOISE.

body forward from these anchor points.

Although some snakes give the impression of fast movement, it is in fact an illusion. Except for short bursts, most snakes cannot keep up with a man walking at a normal brisk pace—4 mph (6.4 kph,) and a human hand can snatch an object faster than most snakes can strike.

The fastest-moving land snake in the world is the slender black mamba, which is found south of the Sahara Desert, Africa. It has been timed moving at a speed of 7 mph (11 kph) over short distances.

A snake sheds its skin regularly as it grows by rubbing its body against a rough surface, such as a tree trunk or a rock. Underneath a new skin is revealed with bright, clean scales.

Some snakes are poisonous.

SNAKES SHED THEIR SKIN IN ONE PIECE, TURNING IT INSIDE OUT AS THEY WRIGGLE OUT.

They have fangs and venom glands. They mostly use their venom to kill prey, although they have been known to use the poison in self-defense, biting an attacker and then injecting venom into the wound. Some vipers are among the most dangerous snakes. The 163 species of viper have large fangs that fold away when not in use. Less than a quarter of all snakes are venomous.

As well as poisonous snakes, constrictors are dangerous too. These giant snakes kill their prey by gripping with their jaws, then wrapping their bodies in tight coils around the victim, stopping them from breathing.

A BABY COBRA IS DEADLY FROM THE TIME IT HATCHES.

In 1996, a giant python was caught near Tenang, Malaysia, coiled around the body of a rubber worker whose head was in its mouth. It had already squeezed him to death. The python was 21 ft (6.6 m) long, 2 1/2 ft (76 cm) in diameter and weighed 309 lb (140 kg.)

Snakes live in many different places: in the sea, underground in burrows, in the desert, even up trees.

Nagas

In Hindu myth, Nagas are a race of serpent demons whose power comes from a jewel embedded in their throats or skulls. Their name means "those who do not walk, who creep." When the gods passed around the cup containing the elixir of immortality, the Nagas grabbed it, but spilled some drops on the ground. As they licked up the drops, the grass split their tongues, which have remained forked ever since.

Unblinking Stare

Snakes have no eyelids. Legend tells that a long time ago, in Australia, Biame, the Good Spirit lived there with all the creatures. Most of the time they lived happily, except when Ngar-ang, the Storm Spirit came by on the back of his Thunderbird. One day, Biame told all the creatures not to look up or open their eyes as Ngar-ang rushed past in the darkness. All the creatures obeyed except the snake, who couldn't resist one quick look. When Ngar-ang saw two bright little eyes shining at him, he swooped down to fight Biame. As a punishment Biame took away the snake's eyelids.

THE "COBRA-GRANDE"

The Amazon, in South America is the largest body of fresh water on Earth. It is also supposedly home to the "cobra-grande," a huge river snake that can swallow deer whole. Since 1906, regular reports have been made of sightings of this monster and wide furrowed tracks have been seen in swamps leading from the river to lakes. At one stage, a team from the National Institute of Amazonian Research went to investigate one sighting, getting there just in time to stop the army from bombing a lake to kill the snake. Despite this, no one has ever seen more than a glimpse of a huge, horned head, or something that creates huge ripples.

Cats

DOMESTIC CATS CAN have special relationships with people. It is sometimes said that cats are the only tame animals that can look a person in the eye without flinching. Despite having a close relationship with humans for over 4,000 years, cats are fiercely independent and must be won over. Only then will they allow their keepers to care for and love them.

Black Cats

In the past, cats were believed to have mystical powers or to be connected with witches, and it is partly because of this that some people still consider cats to be a sign of good luck today. If you meet a black cat and stroke it three times, or if one runs across your path it brings good fortune, and if a black cat comes uninvited into your house you should never chase it away. However, if a black cat walks across the stage during a theater performance, it is said to bring disaster.

The Egyptians worshiped the cat goddess Bastet. Her annual festival was a national celebration.

THERE IS AN OLD English proverb that reads: "In the eyes of a cat all things belong to cats." Cats come and go as they please, when they please, and if neglected may move on to someone more worthy of their affections. However when love is truly given by a cat, it will follow its owner to the ends of the Earth.

THE ROMANS SAW THE CAT AS A SYMBOL OF LIBERTY.

Cats are loners, solitary hunters who roam the dark, mysterious world of twilight and pre-dawn. Even a cat that likes to sit on a window sill and stare out at the world for days on end will suddenly respond to the call of the wild and venture out, maybe to mark its territory in relation to that of neighboring cats. A cat

A CAT STANDS ITS FUR ON END TO MAKE ITSELF LOOK BIGGER.

living in the wild needs a territory in which to catch food, so the bigger this area the better. Although domestic cats do not have this keen sense of survival, the instinct to claim territory still remains, especially for male cats, called toms, who may establish a territory ten times larger than that of female cats, called queens. Two cats in one house will also establish their own "territories," their own areas within the house.

Like their huge relation, the lion, cats use their energy in short bursts and spend a great deal of time sleeping: curled up if cold, or stretched out if warm and relaxed.

WHEN A CAT IS FRIGHTENED ITS PAWS SWEAT.

Unlike the lion, who eats about once a week, cats like to eat a few small meals throughout the day. Any change of routine can cause them to lose their appetite for a while.

Cats communicate with their whole

Cats make good pets. They are clean, independent, and love to sit on your lap!

Cats' Eyes

During the day a cat's pupils are narrow slits, but after dark they open wide to let in as much light as possible. A cat's night vision is six times more sensitive than a human's. Cats' eyes glow in the dark because of a special layer of cells at the back of the eyes, which reflect light just like a mirror.

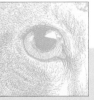

MAN'S BEST FRIENDS?

A man in the German town of Magdenburg used to stroke and talk to a stray cat he passed every day on his way to work. One morning in 1944, during World War II, he was shaving when he heard a cat mewing at the door. On the step was the stray cat. The cat was agitated and rubbed up against the man and seemed to want him to leave the house. The man left, and the cat led him about $\frac{1}{2}$ mile (0.8 km) away, looking back all the while, to check he was still following. Suddenly, overhead, came the roar of the Royal Air Force Lancaster bombers and then the terrible sound of bombs. The man's house was flattened, but the stray cat had saved his life.

Cats enjoy prowling in gardens and fields.

bodies. For example, a cat pricks its ears forward when alert or out hunting, twitches them when nervous, or lays them flat against its head if very frightened or aggressive. If a cat gently flicks its tail it is showing pleasure if relaxed, or readiness to pounce if hunting, but if it starts to thrash its tail around it is indicating anger.

Manx Cats

Manx cats have no tails and it is said they are native to the Isle of Man. Legend has it that invaders of the island cut off the tails to decorate their helmets. Mother cats, to save their kittens from harm, bit off their tails at birth until, eventually, the kittens were born tailless. However, it is more likely that Manx cats were imported from Phoenician traders or entered aboard ships from the Spanish Armada in the sixteenth century.

Dogs

A BOVE ALL OTHER domesticated animals dogs show humankind a spirit of unconditional love and loyalty. They have been man's faithful friends and companions throughout recorded history, often giving their lives in causes not their own, such as when dogs are used by police forces or in times of war. A dog can truly be called "man's best friend."

Argus

The ancient Greek hero, Odysseus went to war while his dog, Argus, was still a puppy. The dog grew and served other men until he was old, neglected, and cast out to sleep on a dunghill. When Odysseus eventually came home, this is where he found his beloved dog. Argus, too feeble to move, wagged his tail—and died of joy. He had waited twenty years and saw his master again at last.

St. Bernards are a large breed of dog used mainly as rescue dogs in mountainous areas.

DOGS ARE THE descendants of wolves and coyotes—they are wild dogs that have been domesticated, and are most like their wild cousins when they howl. Careful breeding over thousands of years has created the several hundred breeds of dog

A DOG STICKS OUT ITS TONGUE AND PANTS TO COOL DOWN.

that exist today.

Throughout the ages dogs have been bred or trained to do different things: herd sheep and cattle, hunt, kill, or retrieve game, and work as police dogs or dogs to help the blind. Others are guard dogs or bred for use in sports such as greyhound racing, or chosen for their natural hardiness to pull sledges in lands of ice and snow,

A DOG WALKS ON TIPTOES— ON THE ENDS OF ITS FEET.

or used by shepherds as "living blankets" on cold nights out on the mountains.

In many, many ways the dog has been of service to humankind over the years, and as a result each variety of breed has qualities that are unique to them: some love water, some need to run miles and miles

Dogs love exercise and need to be walked at least once a day.

DOGS CAN IDENTIFY ONE MOLECULE OF SCENT IN A MILLION.

a walk is suggested, or if it is let off the lead to run free. A dog does not pretend. Leaping, running, and barking are all real expressions of the joy it is feeling at that moment.

A dog also feels shame when it has done something wrong. Often a dog knows its human family will be angry at it, and greets them crouched low and with its head down as a sign of submission. A dog's willingness to love, even when cruelly treated, is amazing. It takes a lot to break its spirit.

A dog's greatest gift is its faithfulness and loyalty, often to the point of self-sacrifice. Jane

Beddgelert

Beddgelert, a small village in Wales, U.K., derived its name from an old legend. The story tells of Prince Llywelyn who left his faithful hound, Gelert, looking after his son, while he went out hunting. On his return to the lodge, he was met by Gelert, his mouth and paws dripping with blood. Horrified the prince saw his baby's crib was overturned and the child missing. The prince drove his sword into Gelert and killed him. Then, hearing a faint cry, he found the baby safe, but beside it the dead body of a wolf, killed by Gelert to save the child. Deeply distressed, the prince buried Gelert and placed a carved stone over the grave so that all would know of his bravery.

each day, some prefer cold weather, others a warm climate.

A dog's strongest sense is smell and one of the things it loves to do is roll. Sometimes if it rolls in something that to us smells foul, it seems as if to the dog it is a double pleasure! If a dog comes home covered in muck it has

DOGS WERE FIRST DOMESTICATED IN THE STONE AGE.

probably had the dog equivalent of a day at the fun fair!

Many people believe dogs have second sight and can predict death. This may be because the human body goes through chemical changes when near to death and dogs can smell these chemical changes.

If anyone thinks animals do not have emotions, they only have to watch a dog showing unrestrained joy and delight when its owners return after a trip away, when

CHIHUAHUAS ARE NAMED AFTER THE STATE OF CHIHUAHUA IN MEXICO.

ALSATIAN SAVIOUR

During World War II, a watchman at the naval air-base of De Kooy, Netherlands, had his attention attracted one day by an Alsatian. The large dog came to the gate, whined and scraped his paw on the ground, and then ran off. The dog repeated this action every ten minutes or so. Eventually the watchman followed the dog and was led to a seriously injured dog nearby, which had obviously been run over by a car. Once the Alsatian knew help had come, it began to lick the other dog's wounds, and stood over the dog when it started to rain. The Dutch Society for the Protection of Animals took both dogs in as they seemed to be strays.

was a dog who was devoted to her owner, Brian. One day, Brian, went climbing, leaving Jane by his jacket and telling her to "stay." While climbing, Brian fell and was taken to hospital. When he woke, he had amnesia and couldn't recall anything. Fifteen days later, his memory returned and he remembered Jane, who he had left waiting by his coat. When he found her she was still there, almost dead, standing on guard where he had left her.

Feeding Habits

A dog will usually eat until full. There are, however, stories of dogs who rise above this basic instinct. One story tells of a female hound dog who fell into a rock crevasse in Tennessee, U.S. without its owners knowing. A male dog, who lived in the same house, ate only a small amount of his food each day, then gathered up the rest and ran off. When rescuers found the bitch ten days later, it was obvious the male dog had been dropping his food into the crevasse to feed her.

Life for mountain gorillas is relatively peaceful, although leaders occasionally have to drive hopeful intruders away from their females.

Apes

WE LIKE TO THINK we are very different to animals, but when it comes to the great apes it is obvious we are very closely related. In fact, chimpanzees are almost 99 percent genetically identical to us. Like us, apes form strong family groups, are intelligent, have feelings and emotions, and use tools.

THE APES— GORILLAS, chimpanzees, gibbons, and orang-utans are all primates. Gorillas are the largest primates, and because of their size and great strength they have often been labeled as stupid and dangerously fierce. This is not true. They are slow, gentle, and intelligent creatures that form close relationships. Mountain gorillas live in groups that usually include a single adult male, one or two immature males, two to four adult females, and two to five young gorillas under eight years old. They travel slowly through

AN ADULT MALE GORILLA CAN WEIGH AS MUCH AS 595 LB (270 KG.)

KOKO KNOWS OVER 1,000 SIGNED WORDS AND UNDERSTANDS OVER 2,000 SPOKEN WORDS.

the forest, eating food before moving on to another feeding ground.

Chimpanzees live in groups of varying sizes: sometimes just males, females with young, or mixed groups. They often fight with neighboring chimpanzee groups. A group's home area depends on its size, but usually it lives deep in the forests or on open grassland. Of all the apes, chimpanzees remind us most of ourselves because of the facial expressions they make and the way they play games, solve puzzles, and make and use tools.

Apes cannot make the sounds of human speech, but they are capable of understanding spoken languages and some have learned to use a sign language. Koko, the famous gorilla, has been using it for 25 years. Both Koko and

CHIMPANZEES ARE THE MOST INTELLIGENT OF ALL ANIMALS.

a chimpanzee called Lana have invented their own words for things. For example, Lana calls a duck a "water-bird" and Koko calls a ring a "finger-bracelet." In April 1998, Koko took part in a live conversation

Mountain gorillas spend their time eating plant food and ranging their home territory, which can be 4–15 square miles (10–39 km².)

Orang-utans spend most of their time high up in trees searching for fruit, shoots, or insects.

via the Internet (a typist keyed in Koko's signed conversation.) The entire 45-minute "chat" was video-taped.

Through the use of this sign language, apes are changing the way we see them. We have assumed that because animals cannot express their feelings in language, they do not have those feelings. Now we know that for some species at least, that is not the case. They are our kin.

Declaration on Apes

The "*Declaration on Great Apes*" was first published in 1993. It sets out a declaration of rights for apes and equality beyond humanity. The declaration states, among other things, that apes should not be killed, except in very strict circumstances, such as self-defense, that humans should protect apes' liberty and not imprison them arbitrarily, and that apes should not be tortured by deliberate infliction of severe pain. It is hoped the declaration will play an important role in producing required social change.

Clever Chimps

Some years ago, scientists at the University of Pennsylvania, Philadelphia, U.S., demonstrated that chimpanzees had a concept of number, including fractions, and could match up completely different types of objects in which the only factor in common was a mathematical similarity. Today, at the Ohio State University, U.S., Sarah Boyson is discovering exactly the same ability in her chimpanzees.

CHILD RESCUE

On August 16, 1996 a three-year-old boy fell 18 ft (5.5 m) into the gorilla enclosure at Brookfield Zoo in Jersey, U.S. All six gorillas rushed to help, but first on the scene was Binti Jua (Swahili for "Daughter of Sunshine") with her own 17-month-old baby clinging to her back. She gently picked up the boy, cradled him in her lap, then carried him across the compound to the human access door, and laid him down so the keepers could rescue him. Binti is the niece of the famous gorilla Koko. Binti was taken from her own mother at birth and sent to San Francisco Zoo, U.S. when she was just three months old.

Celebrations

As humans, we all celebrate certain rituals that traditionally follow the calendar year. We hold many different festivals throughout the year for example, New Year, birthdays, and anniversaries of certain events. We know from the Bible that birthdays were first celebrated at least 4,000 years ago.

Human Evolution

Early in the twentieth century, when scientists were deciding how the human species evolved, they looked at the shape of the human skull and compared it with the fossilized skulls of our distant relatives. They believed it was probable that we evolved from ape-like ancestors, and were much smaller, with longer arms and more body hair than we have today. However, recent research suggests that prehuman apes that walked on two legs had evolved by four million years ago.

Religion and Belief

People have always searched for explanations of why certain events in our lives occur. Religion is a set of beliefs that tries to explain the aspects of life we do not fully understand. There have been and still are a number of different religions in the world—religions whose followers believe in many gods, and other religious groups that worship just one God. Today the main religious groups are: Muslims, Christians, Hindus, Buddhists, and Jews.

Humankind

O NE OF THE LAST SPECIES of mammals to appear on the planet, we are the most successful and dominant alive. Our intelligence has made us capable of incredible achievements: we are the only primate to have developed oral language and technology. We have an insatiable thirst for knowledge, and our understanding of the world and universe about us grows as our species evolves.

AS HUMANS, WE ARE BY far the most numerous and successful of all the primates. In the last 300 years, our population has grown from about 1,000 million to nearly 6,000 million. Because we have intelligent, reasoning minds and opposable thumbs, we have been able to make and use tools and have created a reading and writing system that allows us to communicate in astonishingly complex ways. Through science and technology we are able to make sense of the world about us, and it has taken us four million years to gain all the skills necessary to bring us to where we are today.

More than any other animal, we feel a need to be creative, to express an awareness of ourselves and our surroundings. We have invented tools and devices that help us live our lives as fully and with as much

MOST PRIMATES HAVE LARGE BRAINS AND ARE HIGHLY INTELLIGENT.

enjoyment as possible. Everyone is unique and individual in their interests, which is why we have philosophers, politicians, and sages, athletes, sailors, and mountaineers.

We are capable of feeling and expressing a vast array of emotions, from inconsolable grief, to immense joy. We have huge capacities for compassion and

Humans live all over the planet, from the freezing polar regions to the scorching deserts of Africa.

empathy, and mostly strive to improve life. However, we are also more destructive than any other species alive. War, conflict,

MOTHER TERESA

There are many outstanding people who have dedicated their lives to others, Mother Teresa is one of them. Born Agnes Gonxita Bojaxhiu in a village in Skopje, Macedonia, she joined the Catholic Order of Our Lady of Loreto in 1929, and went on to become one of the best-loved and most well-known workers for the underprivileged on the planet. She became known as "Mother Teresa," and as the Dalai Lama said was "a towering embodiment of the power of love, her great compassion an inspiring example of the true essence and potential of spiritual life." Mother Teresa was awarded the Nobel Peace Prize in 1979. She died in 1997.

HUMANS ARE ALL MEMBERS OF ONE SPECIES CALLED "HOMO SAPIENS."

and argument are part of our daily lives as we struggle to understand and communicate with other humans. Our attempts to live alongside the rest of the animal kingdom are no better: rather than treat them with respect, we often try to own or control them.

THE HUMAN BODY IS A COMPLEX COLLECTION OF MORE THAN 50,000 MILLION LIVING CELLS.

People and Science

We constantly ask questions about our environment: how things are made, why things happen the way they do, where things come from or go to. As a result of this inquiring existence, we have been able to discover all sorts of answers. For example, what the tiniest particles are that make up the universe, how to light our homes with electricity, how to cure diseases, and how to make gadgets to make our lives easier. One of the greatest and most inspirational achievements of humankind was the space voyage of 1969, when Neil Armstrong became the first person to walk on the Moon.

Winter Coats

Our winter anoraks and jackets are often filled with light, airy padding. Heat travels very slowly through still air, so our body heat finds it difficult to escape and keeps us warm instead. A deer's winter coat works in exactly this way. Each hair on its body is hollow, like a small sealed tube, trapping the air to keep it warm. The hair also acts like a life belt in case it needs to swim.

Nimrod

Thousands of years ago, in Mesopotamia, lived a king called Nimrod. Nimrod had twin sons. Out hunting one day, his sons met a beautiful horned doe (female deer,) whose antlers glittered with light. They chased the doe for two days until she jumped into a lake and disappeared. In sadness Nimrod's sons built a temple by the lake and lived in it for five years.

Reindeer Facts

Reindeer live in the vast stretches of icy tundra across the top of the world. A reindeer oddity is that it has a loose tendon, which slips over the ankle bone, making a loud clicking sound as the animal walks. The reindeer is the only species in which both males and females grow antlers. A baby reindeer's antlers start to grow at three weeks.

Deer

DEER ARE CREATURES of paradox—graceful, sensitive, and gentle, yet also very determined to follow their own paths. Deer have an amazing ability to freeze on the spot and often camouflage themselves against their surroundings. There are many tales of deer luring hunters deep into the forest, and then simply melting away into the trees.

THERE ARE ABOUT 36 different types of deer and they are found on every continent. Different species have adapted to all climates from tropical to polar.

The most obvious characteristic of deer is their pair of antlers, which only the males possess. Antlers are covered with a fur called velvet, which feeds blood to the antlers as they grow. Once

LIKE ALL DEER, CARIBOUS ARE HERBIVORES. THEY EAT LEAVES, LICHENS, AND FINE TWIGS.

a year, adult males fight with their antlers to decide which of them will mate with the females. During the fight, called the rut, the male spends his time roaring loudly. Deer shed their antlers each spring and grow new ones in time for the next rutting season.

For centuries, deer have been hunted, but they have developed many ways to survive. When in danger, the sika deer fluffs up the patch of white fur

White tailed deer are shy animals that do not usually congregate in large herds.

CHINESE WATER DEER ARE THE ONLY DEER NOT TO HAVE ANTLERS.

on its rump as a warning signal to other deer. In summer, the fallow deer has white spots on its coat, which provide a clever camouflage against leaves and branches.

A deer has an excellent sense of hearing. Instead of moving the whole of its head, it swivels the outer parts of its ears to locate

THE ELK, OR MOOSE, IS THE LARGEST OF ALL THE DEER.

the sound. This enables it to listen while feeding, and also to know immediately from which direction the sound is coming

The Long Trek

In Alaska and northern Canada, reindeer are called caribou. The caribou of Canada make the longest migrations of any land mammal. Their young are born in the high tundra of the Arctic during the summer months and then, in the autumn, herds of up to 20,000 deer move south 700 miles (1,125 km) to the edge of the forest region. In the summer they go back north, a round trip of 1,400 miles (2,250 km.)

THE FAWN'S SPOTS

When the first ever fawn was born, its mother was nervous. All around her, watching from the shadows were fierce animals that preyed on the young and the weak. So she prayed to the Great Creator to find some way to protect her child with its weak and wobbly legs. The Creator put down his work and came. He made the fawn a shirt of soft doe skin, dabbed with the colors of the brown earth and the black fire charcoal, and added some white, yellow, and just a touch of red, saying, "As long as the fawn wears this and keeps still, he will be invisible to all his enemies." From that day onward if a fawn remains absolutely still, it is camouflaged by its dappled coat.

and flee. A deer's whole survival depends on the sensitivity of its ears.

Musk deer have special glands under their stomachs, which produce a smelly substance, called musk, during the breeding season. Many have been hunted and killed to obtain this gland, which is then used to make perfume.

The pampas deer has similar glands on his hooves, which give off a strong garlicky smell that can be detected 1 mile (1.6 km) away.

King of Benares

An old Indian story tells of two herds of deer, each led by a golden stag, Branch and King Banyan, living in a royal park. Each day the King of Benares visited the park and killed many of the deer. Unhappy, the stags decided that every day the deer should draw lots. Whoever drew the lot would be sacrificed to save the others. One day the lot fell on a pregnant doe. King Banyan graciously offered to die in her place. When the King of Benares heard this he was so touched he never hunted the deer again.

Rabbits and hares

ALTHOUGH RABBITS AND HARES ARE members of the same family, rabbits have been domesticated and bred as family pets, but hares have always remained wild. They both have huge hind limbs, which make them very swift runners, and chisel-shaped teeth, which grow throughout their lives. Rabbits and hares are often seen in meadows at dusk, and because of this they are often linked with the Moon.

RABBITS AND HARES have some very different physical characteristics. The hare is much larger than the rabbit, having a body length of $20^1/_2$–$23^1/_2$ in (52–59.5 cm) to the rabbit's 16 in (40 cm.) Its ears are much larger, and its hind legs more powerful.

Most of a hare's and a rabbit's body heat is lost through its ears, and the size varies according to whether the animal lives in a hot

IF SNOW HAS COVERED THE GROUND AND THERE IS NO GRASS TO EAT RABBITS EAT TREE BARK.

or cold climate—the Jack rabbit of Arizona, U.S. has very large ears, whereas the ears of the Arctic hare are small.

Rabbits can be found almost anywhere as they burrow out their homes and tunnels in the earth. Their burrow system is called a warren, where up to 30 rabbits live in a social group. Baby rabbits (called kittens,) are born blind, deaf, and hairless in a side burrow lined with their

Hare Council

The hares were afraid. Surrounded by enemies—men, dogs, beasts, and birds of prey—they lacked courage to go on. So they called a council and at length decided they would all kill themselves. As the hares rushed toward a nearby pool to drown themselves, they frightened the frogs who jumped into the water and hid beneath lily pads. The hares were so pleased to find a creature that was actually frightened of them, they decide to live on a little longer.

Hare Tales

The children's tales of Brer Rabbit come from the West African belief in the hare as a trickster. The hare was also seen as a trickster by the plainsmen of North America. If you meet a hare it is generally considered to be unlucky, and if one crosses your path, it is best to go home again.

Story of Snowshoes

Snowshoe hares have thick white hair on their feet to stop them from sinking into the snow. One story tells how the hare got his snowshoes. When the world was young and Michabou the mighty hunter fought the Spirit-Bear to see who would be king of the north, the hare helped the Spirit-Bear by stealing Michabou's snowshoes as he lay sleeping. When Michabou woke he could no longer walk across the deep snow, but sank. In the end he grew tired and gave up the battle. As a reward, Spirit-Bear let the hare keep the snowshoes.

mother's fur. Their eyes open at 10 days, and at 18 days they start to play outside. Rabbits are very alert to danger and can even be startled by their own shadows. Their huge ears help them pick up even the smallest of sounds.

AS AN ALARM SIGNAL, RABBITS THUMP THEIR HIND FEET HARD ON THE GROUND.

Hares are more solitary than rabbits and live in more exposed countryside. They do not burrow, but live in forms. A form is a shallow bowl that the hare scrapes in the ground among long grass.

Rabbits and hares have a good defense instinct—when a shadow passes by, they can freeze in an instant, so avoiding the keen eye of a bird of prey flying overhead, but they can also run fast,

SOME RABBITS CAN HAVE UP TO 30 BABIES IN ONE YEAR.

Easter Hare

The pagan goddess of spring was the hare-headed Eastre. Her favorite animal was, naturally, the hare and it was the first animal to be linked with the Easter festival. Later the rabbit became linked too. German children are told the Easter hare lays the Easter eggs they receive each year. This may be because a bird called a plover lays its eggs in an empty hare's form.

BREEDING RABBITS

In 1850, British settlers took six rabbits to Australia. The rabbits bred and spread out across Australia at the rate of 70 miles (110 km) a year. By the end of the century, rabbits had changed the face of Australia, eating most of the shrubs and grasses, and leaving much of the countryside looking like a dust bowl. Ranchers put up fences to keep the rabbits out, but there were so many of them that when they came to a fence, those at the rear climbed on the backs of those at the front and climbed over the fence! In 1950, Australians introduced the terrible disease myxomatosis to kill the swarming rabbits and give the grasses a chance to grow again.

twisting and doubling back to avoid being caught. A hare can run at 45 mph (70 kph.)

ARCTIC HARES AND SNOWSHOE HARES GROW WHITE FUR IN THE WINTER TO BLEND IN WITH THE SNOW.

Hares and rabbits come out of their forms and burrows just as the moon is rising, and spend a few hours frolicking around as the night draws in.

Hares and Witches

During the Middle Ages it was thought a witch could change into a hare and if a hare was wounded then a witch would be found with a similar injury. In fact, one woman accused of witchcraft in 1662, recited at her trial:
"I shall go intill a hare,
With sorrow and sych meikle care.
And I shall go in the Devil's name,
Ay when I come home again."

Rats

R ATS HAVE LONG been seen as enemies of humans. Many people dislike the sight of them as they often carry diseases: the bubonic plague that spread across Europe in the 1300s and killed 25 million people, a quarter of the population of Europe, was carried by rats traveling in the holds of ships sailing from the Black Sea to Genoa.

Blind Leading Blind

In 1924, a miner noticed two rats walking, one slightly behind the other, each holding one end of a piece of straw in its mouth. After watching for a while, he realized that the second rat was blind and was being led by the first. A naturalist, taking part in the BBC's Living World program reported that he had seen two rats walking along, one holding the tail of the other. When he examined the rats, the tail-holding rat was blind in both eyes.

Rats can become serious pests, devouring huge quantities of crops.

THERE ARE MORE than 50 species of wild rat, living in most terrain from damp places to deserts. Most rats use burrows, but some live in buildings and some even live in trees. Rats will eat almost anything and can gnaw their way through most materials. Their diet includes birds' eggs, garbage, cloth, dead animals, and farm crops. In one test at the Public Health Service Laboratory in Savannah, U.S., rats chewed through a

RATS' FRONT TEETH STAY PERMANENTLY SHARP.

panel of foam glass 2 in (5 cm) thick, and a panel of aluminum $1/2$ in ($1^1/4$ cm) thick.

Rats have a strong family urge and female rats will adopt almost any animal given the chance. Experiments have shown that they will adopt baby mice, rabbits, kittens, and even chicks.

Rats are very intelligent, in fact, they are almost as intelligent as

WHEN A RAT IS RELAXED IT GRITS ITS TEETH.

dogs, and need the company of a social group. They are not often puzzled by the same obstacle twice. Rats are genetically very adaptable and some populations have even become immune to the poison warfarin put down to kill them. Now some rats need to eat warfarin regularly just to survive.

Mice

LIKE RATS, MICE are rodents or "gnawing animals." They have no canine teeth, and there is a wide gap between their incisors and molars so that the incisors can be used for gnawing, nibbling, and carrying. These teeth never stop growing, so rodents need to wear them down by gnawing.

ALTHOUGH EQUALLY adaptable to their surroundings, mice are more cautious than rats. A mouse will use his whiskers to measure a space before he tries to squeeze through. Mice are constantly alert to danger, scampering swiftly and silently from one piece of cover to

The harvest mouse is so light it can climb a wheat stalk without bending it.

THE MOUSE AND THE GIRAFFE HAVE THE SAME NUMBER OF NECK BONES—SEVEN.

another, but if faced with an enemy they have tremendous courage, despite their size.

Like rats, mice breed at an astonishing rate. They are mature at 10 to 12 weeks, and a single mouse may have 30 or 40 young in the course of a year. If these all survive and have children themselves, in two years a pair of mice could be ancestors of a million offspring.

WHITE TAME MICE ARE DOMESTICATED VARIETIES OF WILD MICE.

Mice and rats may live in dirty places, but they keep themselves clean, stopping to groom their coats regularly, even when hunting. They are good house keepers and store up food for the future.

The common house mouse is about 4 in (10 cm) long with a tail of around $4^1/_2$ in (11 cm) and lives in houses, barns, and similar places. The tiny harvest mouse is only $2^1/_2$ in (6 cm) long, with a tail about the same length.

Dormice easily fit into the palm of a hand. They live mainly in hedgerows, but as they only come out at night, it is not likely that you will often see one.

Strong Mice

The word "muscle" comes from the Latin word, *musculus* meaning "little mouse." If you hold one arm out straight, palm up, clench your fist and then bend your arm up and down at the elbow, you should be able to see the biceps muscles moving about like a little mouse under your skin.

SUPER MOUSE

H.C. Hahn, a biologist from Texas, U.S. tells the story of a brave mouse. Once, while on wildlife trip, he saw a snake climbing a tree with a field mouse in its mouth. As he watched, suddenly another mouse ran up the tree and jumped on the snake's back, sinking its teeth in and hanging on grimly. Unable to attack the second mouse as it still had the first in its mouth, the snake dropped its prey and turned on the hero. As soon as the second mouse saw that its companion had been released, it leapt off the snake's back, escaping just before the snake had a chance to strike again, and ran for safety with its mate.

Ant Bodyguards

Some black ants act as bodyguards for the caterpillar of the imperial blue butterfly. Each morning, the ants leave their underground nests and climb wattle trees to join the caterpillars as they eat the leaves. The ants use their strong jaws to drive off any predators, while the caterpillars feed. As payment, the ants get to suck a sugary secretion from the caterpillars' backs.

Circular Milling

When ants are on the march or attack, sometimes those on the edges of the columns get cut off from the others. They seem to lose their sense of direction, then and begin to go round in circles. Hundreds or even thousands of ants continue this circular milling for days until they die.

Leaf-cutter ants carry home leaf pieces to their nests to help cultivate the fungi they use for food.

Ants and termites

BOTH ANTS AND termites are extremely social animals—in one nest there can be several thousand ants or termites. The welfare of the group is put above that of each individual, and throughout their lives, most ants and termites work very hard, each member of the group having its own particular job to fulfil. Co-operation and industry sums up the lives of these little creatures.

ANTS LIVE IN HIGHLY organized colonies consisting of winged males, wingless females (called workers,) and fertile females (called queens.) Male ants have wings and short antennae, and their only job is to mate with the queen. Once they have done this they die. Queens do not work, but breed to produce the offspring for the colony. Most worker ants carry out their role without ever stopping for a rest,

collecting materials for nest building and food for the rest of the group.

Ants can carry many times their own size in weight, and if the item they find is too heavy for them, they will drag it or get

THERE ARE AT LEAST 10,000 BILLION ANTS IN THE WORLD.

help from other workers. If an obstacle is in their path, they will either march over it, round it, or even take it with them.

Some ants have slaves to do some of the work for them. For example, the British red ant and the European Amazon ant raid the nests of

WOOD ANTS BUILD MOUNDS OF PLANT DEBRIS THAT CAN REACH 5 FT (1.5 M) HIGH.

The central royal chamber, where the queen lays her eggs, is at the heart of a termite mound.

honeydew. When the plants start to wilt, the ants move the aphids to new plants, just like a farmer moves his cows to new pasture!

Most termites are the size of

THERE ARE AROUND 2,000 SPECIES OF TERMITES IN THE WORLD.

a grain of rice, almost blind, and sterile. They live in colonies, just like ants, with the queen laying up to 36,000 eggs a day. When the colony is big enough, the queen starts to produce winged males and females that fly away to start new colonies.

Termites build high-rise dwellings called termitaries. Inside these pillars of soil cemented with saliva and

black ants and carry off the pupae to their own nests. When the new ants are born, they become slaves.

Some ants keep their own "cattle"—tiny aphids or greenfly which produce a sticky substance called honeydew.

baked by the Sun, are layers of rooms, galleries, and passageways, with ventilation and drainage. In some parts of Africa and Australia, termitaries reach 20 ft (6 m) high and are 10 ft (3 m) in diameter. They are home to around three million termites.

The ants herd the aphids together and "milk" them. In the autumn, the ants collect the aphids' eggs and watch over them until they hatch in spring. Then the ants carry the aphids above ground to allow them to suck the sap from plants and so produce some more

Which Way?

Dr. Felix Santschi, a zoologist, demonstrated that ants navigate by observing the position of the Sun. First he covered traveling ants with lightproof boxes so that they were completely in the dark. Then he removed and replaced the boxes intermittently. Each time the box was removed, the ants set off on a different course, altered by the degree in which the Sun had moved while they were kept in the dark.

Leaf-cutter ants have huge jaws that operate like shears as they slice the leaves into manageable pieces for transport.

MEXICAN ARMY ANTS

Some ants will eat their way through anything. Mexican army ants, although blind, divide into columns to encircle their prey. Now ants are on the march in Brazil—but these are not ordinary, "eat-anything-that-gets-in-the-way ants." These ants have developed a taste for the protective gel that coats computer circuit boards. They are also partial to televisions, telephone circuitry, and anything else that contains a computer circuit board. Some ants even ate through the wiring of the world's largest superconductor while it was still under construction and short-circuited the system. So keep crumbs away from your computer—they might attract ants!

Super senses

ANIMALS ARE PROBABLY much better at reading our body signals than we are at reading theirs. The development and use of senses varies widely from species to species, but recent research shows that many animals see, hear, smell, and sense far more than humans can. Across the animal kingdom are creatures who can see farther than us, see more of the light spectrum than we can, hear higher and lower sounds, and have a sense of taste that is far more subtle than ours.

A wolf's pointed snout encourages air to circulate around the the sensory cells inside.

Smell

At the top of your nose is a small patch of tissue with thousands of smell sensors. Nerve fibres take messages from these sensors to the brain. A wolf needs all its senses to be keen, but relies mainly on hearing and smell when hunting. Its sense of smell is 100 times greater than that of a human.

Snakes do not have separate senses of taste and smell.

Taste

Taste buds, situated on your tongue, are sensitive to different types of chemicals dissolved in your saliva, which you taste as sweet, salt, sour, or bitter. Taste is linked to smell. A snake tastes by flicking out its tongue and collecting chemicals from the air. It then presses its tongue against the smell center on the roof of its mouth.

Sight

Eyes work together to detect patterns of light and send this information to the brain where it is interpreted to create vision. Powerful eyesight would be little use to a fish, but for a hunting bird, high in the sky, keen sight is essential to spot prey on the ground. A hawk's eyes have about five times as many light-sensitive cells as a human's.

Touch

Touch receptors are scattered over the entire surface of the human body. A fish has cells that are sensitive to touch along each side of the body. Together the cells form the lateral line, which is sensitive to vibrations in the water caused by other fish and plants. Some fish can even detect minute electrical charges in the water.

Grasshoppers can pick up high-frequency chirps using receptors on their legs.

Sound

You collect sounds through your ears. The outer ear collects the sound waves and sends them on to vibrate against the ear drum, where they are converted into nerve messages that run to the brain. A grasshopper's sound sensors are on its abdomen, where its hind legs join the body.

Pets and people

FOR MANY PEOPLE, a pet is their first contact with an animal, and through this relationship they learn to love and respect a member of a different species. A pet will show great affection for and loyalty to its human companion, sometimes to the point of sacrificing its life for that person. In return, we should get to know its nature and its needs, and give it the company and support it would get in its own family group.

History of pets

Humans have kept pets for at least 4,000 years. The first pets were tamed, wild animals, especially the big cats like lions and hyenas. The ancient Egyptians were especially fond of cats. When their cats died, they mummified them and buried them in special tombs.

Caring for a pony every day can be hard work, but also very rewarding and lots of fun.

Famous pets

Many famous people have had pet cats. Charles Dickens, the Brontë sisters, Dr. Johnson, and T.S. Eliot, all owned and wrote about their pet cats. In the 7th century, the prophet Mohammed was recorded to have cut off the sleeve of his coat to avoid disturbing his sleeping cat. In the 18th century, Queen Marie of France, wife of King Louis XVI, decreed that cats should have the freedom of the city of Paris.

Fun with your pet

If you follow these ground rules, your pet will reward you with love and trust, and you will learn the fun and joy to be found in coming to know and care for another creature.

1) Never ever hit your pet—even to tell it off.
2) Never tease your pet or allow anyone else to tease it.
3) Spend time with your pet every day, and be sensitive to its physical and emotional needs.
4) Don't expect "human" reactions.
5) Make sure your pet is not bored or lonely.

Owning a pet

A pet is not a toy. It is a living creature like yourself that can also feel hungry, afraid, and hurt. Before you choose a pet, consider first how much space an animal will need, and how much time, energy, and expense it will take to look after it properly.

- Remember, a cute young creature will grow into a larger one.
- Find out what vaccinations and health certificates an animal will need.
- NEVER acquire a pet on an impulse or as a gift from someone.

Ponies

Owning a pony is a very large responsibility, but you may be able to share the chores with someone else. A pony must be kept in a stable overnight, and turned out into a field during the daytime. Part of your daily routine will involve mucking out, grooming, and riding your pony.

Dogs

Never buy a dog if it will be chained up or left alone all day. Dogs are pack animals and need company, kindness, exercise, firm leadership, and patient handling. In return a dog will give you loyalty and affection. Rightly treated, a dog will become a firm friend and companion for life.

Cats

Cats are popular pets because they are clean, affectionate, intelligent, enjoy human company, but are independent. Handle them gently, provide a warm place for them to sleep, toys for them to play with, a toilet box if they cannot get outside. Doctors have found that stroking a cat calms people down and releases stress.

Hamsters

Hamsters love to store food and are good at escaping. Once free, they will chew anything they can get their teeth into. Hamsters are nocturnal by nature, so if you want to see your pet active during the day, this is not the pet for you. Hamsters are solitary creatures that get easily bored and need toys.

Guinea pigs

Guinea pigs are nervous and easily frightened, so they need to be treated very gently. They can be house-trained, but can also be easily stepped on so it is safer to provide them with their own hutch-home. A guinea-pig has eleven different communication sounds and is sociable to other guinea pigs.

Gerbils

Gerbils are social creatures that live in groups, so a gerbil in a cage on its own will be lonely. Gerbils can jump five times their own height, and like to dig and burrow, so a deep-tank, half-filled with peat and chopped straw, with a wire mesh roof is an ideal home.

Rabbits

Rabbits are cute-looking animals. Their long ears and silky fur make them lovely to stroke. Rabbits need a good-sized, clean hutch in which to live. It can be kept outside during the summer, but needs to be brought inside when the weather turns cold. Rabbits like running and a spacious rabbit run will make them happy.

Mice

Mice like human company, and enjoy sitting on human hands while being stroked gently and talked to softly. Mice need fresh food and clean water daily, and their cage and water bottle should be cleaned each week.

Fish

Fish make fascinating pets. They are clean and quiet, and take up very little space—even a tiny flat has room for a fish tank. Fish need very little attention, but will provide hours of pleasure as you watch them swim around their watery world. Tropical fish come in many beautiful colors.

Rats

Like their wild cousins, domesticated rats are very intelligent. Unlike wild rats, they are clean and affectionate. Rats need plenty of attention and lots to do and explore. Treat it right and a rat will form a loving bond with you and be genuinely excited during family activities.

Trixie

In 1991, Mr. Jack Fyfe, who lives in Sydney, Australia, had a stroke while in bed in his own home. He became paralyzed and was unable to call for help. His sheepdog Trixie found him lying there, and for nine days kept him alive by soaking a towel in her drinking bowl and draping it over her owner's face so he could suck it. When Mr. Fyfe's daughter found him, Trixie was suffering from malnutrition as she had stayed by Mr. Fyfe's bed the whole time.

Animal habitats

EVERYONE NEEDS SOMEWHERE to live. Wild animals make their homes in the forests, marshes, deserts, rivers, and seas of our planet. Different regions of the world have different climates, and this affects the planet's surface in those areas and the life that thrives there. Areas with different physical and chemical features, such as climate and soil type, are homes to different animals and are called habitats.

Tundra and polar

Each summer, the cold polar regions, with their oxygen-rich waters are home to many creatures. A variety of animals come and feed on the Arctic tundra or eat the fish and krill in the seas.

Deserts

On either side of the equator, two bands of desert stretch across the Earth. The most obvious thing about a desert is the lack of water. While the days can be burning hot, night temperatures can drop below freezing point.

North America

Atlantic Ocean

Pacific Ocean

South America

Marshes and swamps

Waterlogged places develop near lakes and rivers and along coastlines. They are usually home to small mammals, crocodiles, birds, fish, snakes, and insects. Saltwater marshes and shores have habitats that change as the tides rise and fall.

Rain forests

A tropical forest only grows near the Equator, where the climate is hot and humid. These forest are home to the richest variety of wildlife, that lives in the trees or burrows in the dark of the decaying plants and leaves on the forest floor.

Forests and woodland

The world's coniferous forests and broad-leaved woodlands are home to many creatures that will have nowhere to go and nothing to eat if we continue to destroy their habitats for wood and land.

Rivers and lakes

Lakes and rivers are found all over the world. These freshwater habitats are home to thousands of different animals and fish.

Mountains

Every continent has mountainous regions. They contain a wide range of habitats including forests on lower slopes, and grassland and tundra farther up. Mountains are home to many creatures, living at different levels.

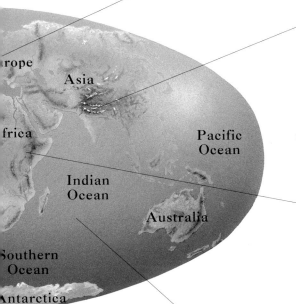

Oceans

A vast ecosystem, with deep underwater valleys and high mountains beneath the sea, the ocean is home to millions of creatures, many of which we know little about. The oceans of the world help regulate the climate for all the other habitats.

Grasslands

All continents have areas of grassland, where it is too dry for most trees to grow. Grasses provide a wonderful food supply as all of the plant can be eaten: the seeds, blades, stalk, and roots.

Air

THE ELEMENT AIR symbolizes communication of thought—the expansion of the mind through the journey of the imagination into music, song, poetry, and truth. This element, which birds and insects can fly through without support, frees our minds to realize new things. The view from here allows us look at creatures from different angles and take delight in their beauty and uniqueness. Read these pages and let your imagination soar with the eagles, look deep into the night with the owls, or wonder at the colors of tropical birds.

THE LARGEST FLYING CREATURES IN HISTORY WERE PTEROSAURS. THEY LIVED 70 MILLION YEARS AGO.

FEATHERS ARE A MASTERPIECE OF NATURE—LIGHT, YET WEIGHT-BEARING AND INSULATING.

BIRDS AND BATS USE THEIR TAILS AS AIR-RUDDERS, TURNING THEM TO CHANGE FLIGHT DIRECTION.

Hanging Out

A bat hooks the curved claws on its hind feet around a support and hangs head downward. In this position, its toes automatically grip the support without slipping. This is because they are pulled by tendons which are stretched by the weight of the bat's body. Even if the bat falls asleep, it will not fall off. In this position, a bat has a good view of what is going on around it and its wings can be spread ready for takeoff.

Chinese Bats

In China, the bat is a symbol of long life and happiness, bringing with it five-fold blessings of wealth, health, virtue, old age, and a natural death. Fu-Xing, the Chinese god of happiness, is often shown as a bat.

There are about 130 different species of fruit-eating bats. They search for fruit in trees using their keen sense of smell.

Bats

BATS ARE THE only true flying mammals. Their wings have very similar bones to the arms and hands of humans, with skin stretched between their long finger bones and bodies, to form the wing membrane. As well as for sustained flight, bats use their wings as blankets while they sleep. Their legs are so weak they can hardly crawl, but their strong wings help them to takeoff into a fast flight from a flat surface.

INSECT-EATING BATS are mainly nocturnal, whereas fruit bats fly during the day or at twilight. When insect-eating bats fly, they send out high-frequency squeaks, mostly inaudible to the human ear. The returning echoes give them information about what is ahead of them, including the size and shape of an object, whether it is moving, and if it is, in which direction. This system of finding

TWENTY-FIVE PERCENT OF ALL MAMMALS ON EARTH ARE BATS.

their way is called echolocation. When flying in groups, bats don't collide as each responds to its own echo-signals.

There are nearly 1,000 species of bat in the world. In fact, one species in every four mammals is a bat. Like all mammals, bats have hair or fur on their bodies, are warm-blooded, and when

THE WORLD'S SMALLEST BAT IS THE HOG-NOSED BAT AT 1¼ IN (3 CM) LONG.

babies, feed on their mother's milk.

Many bats eat insects. The tiny pipistrelle bat can eat 300 mosquitoes in an hour. They pollinate flowers, live in our houses, and fly daily in our evening skies, yet few people see them.

Bats don't make nests,

Pipistrelle bats roost in groups of up to a thousand or more, in lofts, churches, or farm out-buildings.

but find cozy nooks and crannies in which to live. At one time they inhabited caves and hollow trees, but we have cut down so many trees and blocked up so many caves

THE LARGEST FRUIT BAT HAS A WING SPAN OF MORE THAN 4 FT (1 M.)

that more and more bats are making their homes in roof spaces. However, the biggest gatherings of mammals on Earth are still found in the caves of southern U.S., where Mexican free-tailed bats live in colonies of up to 30 million.

Bats that live in colder climates find a quiet place free from disturbance, such as a crack in a rock, and tuck themselves away to hibernate during the winter. They go into hibernation with round, fat stomachs full of food, which keeps them alive through the winter. In spring they emerge very thin and have to find more food quickly to build up their strength.

Vampire Bats

Western belief has always linked bats to vampires—undead spirits which prey on the blood of the living. In the Middle Ages in Europe, people thought bats sucked blood from sleeping children. A vampire bat has four razor-sharp canine teeth with which it collects the blood of other animals, usually horses, and shares it with other bats. Bats starve very quickly, so this "food sharing" saves their lives.

Immortality

As bats live in caves, which were seen as entrances to the next world, they were thought to be immortal and so became symbols of immortality. In parts of Africa, Australia, Bosnia, Tonga, and England, the bat was sacred because it was believed to represent the soul of the dead. Some people even believed that if you touched a bat, your soul would be able to travel at night.

WHITE LADY

Leonard Dubkin, a naturalist, wrote affectionately about the bats he studied. One, called White Lady, once flew straight through an electric fan rotating at the rate of 800 revolutions a minute, without being damaged. Once, as a tiny baby, it was hanging from Dubkin's finger when its mother flew past, grabbed it off the finger, and carried it away without pausing in flight. When White Lady was grown up, to test its homing instinct, Dubkin drove 90 miles (144 km) from his house and released it in country it had never seen. When he got home, White Lady was already there.

Bee Sting

The queen bee is the only bee with a retractable sting. If a worker stings, it leaves the sting in its victim's flesh, and dies. A story from ancient Rome tells how a bee took some honey as a gift to the god Jupiter and Jupiter offered the bee a gift in return. The bee asked for a sting to protect her honey from humans. Jupiter loved the human race, but had made a promise, so said, "You shall have your sting, but at peril of your own life. If you use it, you will die from the loss of it."

Bees collect pollen and store it in pollen sacs on their back legs.

Bees

FIRST APPEARING on the planet 146–174 million years ago, bees have been around on Earth three times longer than the Rocky Mountains, U.S. In ancient Egypt, the bee was said to have sprung from the tears of their Sun god, Ra—in fact, bees do take directional guidance from the Sun. The bee was also seen as a giver of life, because although it seemed to die in the winter, it returned each spring.

EACH INDIVIDUAL honey bee is part of a colony of thousands in the beehive. The focus of each hive is the large queen bee, that lays up to 3,000 eggs a day. To maintain the energy to do this, every 24 hours she eats 80 times her own weight.

BEES SUCK UP NECTAR FROM FLOWERS THROUGH THEIR LONG, HOLLOW TONGUES.

Each cell of honeycomb is six-sided.

Most of the other 20,000–40,000 bees in a hive are workers, females with various tasks. Some are nurses feeding protein-rich bee milk to the queen and the larvae. Some workers make wax, eating honey that is converted by special glands into beeswax, then chewing the wax and moulding it into six-sided honeycomb cells. The cells hold the stores of honey, pollen, or the young larvae. Other workers go out to find pollen and nectar,

FLYING BEES BEAT THEIR WINGS 180 TIMES PER SECOND AND FLY AT A RATE OF 22 MPH (35 KPH.)

which they give to the honeymakers to store in the combs. The older bees act as hive guards. The average life-span of a worker bee is just seven to eight weeks. Males, or drones, exist only to mate with the young queens and then they die.

Wasps

L IKE BEES, social wasps, those that live in colonies, are either queens, drones, or workers. Solitary wasps, those that live alone, are simply males or females. The most common wasp, with its yellow and black body, is a social wasp. It lives in nests made from papery material.

IN EARLY SUMMER, the queen starts a nest by building a few six-sided cells of a comb and laying eggs in each. The nests are made by chewing wood from trees and fences and mixing it to a pulp with saliva. Once the little grubs hatch out, the queen feeds them fruit and flower juices, then whole pieces of fruit or caterpillar. Unlike the queen bee, the queen wasp works from dawn to dusk.

Finally the grubs pupate and produce workers that continue to build the nest into a home for

THE SPIDER-HUNTING WASP OF SOUTH AMERICA IS 2¹/₂ IN (63 MM) LONG.

many more. These wasp nests have rows and rows of neat cells, like a block of flats. Workers clean out each cell as soon as it is empty, ready for the queen to lay another egg.

Wasp drones are not idle either, but share in the work of the nest, cleaning out cells and moving the bodies of dead wasps or grubs. As soon as the colder days of autumn arrive, all the grubs that are left are taken from the cells and killed. This seems cruel, but it saves them from a lingering death as workers will no longer be able

to find food for them. The first frosty night kills the workers and the drones die soon after. Only the queens, hiding in hollow trees

ONE WASPS' NEST CAN EASILY BE HOME TO AROUND 5,000 WASPS.

or under loose bark, live to start a new colony the following year.

Some species of wasp are more likely to sting than others, and generally, smaller wasps are less aggressive than larger ones. Usually a wasp will only sting to defend the nest or if it feels threatened. When a wasp is protecting the nest it flies with a wing beat frequency that rouses other wasps, encouraging them to fly around and attack the intruder.

In summer, wasps are drawn to rotting fruit. They use it as a substitute for nectar, chewing with their powerful mouthparts.

Solitary Wasps

Solitary wasps can be divided into those that use a nest and those that don't. Nest building females construct a few separate cells or dig small holes in the ground and lay one egg in each, next to a paralyzed insect, which is food for hatched larvae. Others lay their eggs in the paralyzed prey so that when the larvae hatch, they can eat their way out of their home.

THE BEE WOLF

The bee wolf is actually a wasp. Mostly yellow in color, the female bee wolf wasp digs an amazing series of tunnels and nest cells in sandy soil, doing most of the digging with her front legs. She feeds her larvae on honey bees, three to six in each of the 15-20 cells. She lays an egg in each cell and seals the doorway with soil. Within three days, the eggs hatch and the larvae start eating. Two weeks later, their food supply used up, the larvae spin a bottle-shaped cocoon and settle down to turn into bee wolf wasps. When they hatch, the wasps have to dig their way out of their cells and into one of the tunnels that leads to the exit from their underground home.

Butterflies and moths

Passionflower

In the tropical forests of Central and South America, a battle is going on between a butterfly and a vine. The heliconus butterfly lays her eggs on the passionflower vines. When the larvae hatch, they eat the vine leaves.

To save themselves, the vines try to fool the butterflies into thinking they are not vines but other plants, by varying the shapes of their leaves. However, the butterfly is not so easily taken in. When it lands on a leaf it drums its legs up and down to test if the leaf actually sounds like a vine leaf.

Moon Madness

Some moths use the Moon like a compass to guide them, so light bulbs and candles will easily distract them. Often a moth flutters into a naked flame by mistake and burns up. Sometimes the moth is seen as a symbol of the soul's mysterious, self-sacrificial love for the divine light.

Too Clean

The pale version of the gray peppered moth is well-camouflaged against lichen on trees and walls. In the 1860s, a black version of the moth appeared. On soot-covered trees and buildings of industrial cities, the dark version was better camouflaged than the original form and became common as it was less likely to be eaten by birds. As city air becomes cleaner, and lichens flourish once more, so the pale version is becoming more common again.

IN THE DAYS of your great grandparents, summer gardens would have been busy and bright with butterflies and moths, living jewels of color, flitting from flower to leaf. Today, the sight of a butterfly or moth is an unexpected bonus and surprise. Modern farming methods have taken over flower-strewn meadows and hedgerows, where butterflies and moths used to feed.

IN CHRISTIAN, CHINESE, Greek, Italian, and Mexican mythology, butterflies and moths, with their life cycle from caterpillar through to chrysalis and winged creature, are symbols of life after death. The Chinese linked butterflies with the Plum Tree of Life and they often buried their dead with jade amulets of carved butterflies.

When you look at a beautiful

BUTTERFLIES CAN TRAVEL UP TO 600 MILES (1,000 KM) WITHOUT STOPPING.

butterfly or moth, there seems no obvious connection between it and a caterpillar. However, it is the slow-moving caterpillar that turns into this delicate, winged creature—one of the most extraordinary transformations on our planet.

The eggs of a butterfly or a moth hatch into caterpillars, which start eating straight away. They munch away for weeks,

THE ANTENNAE OF A MALE MOTH CAN PICK UP THE SCENT OF A FEMALE 5 MILES (8 KM) AWAY.

growing larger and larger and they shed their skins several times. When the caterpillar has reached full size, it ties itself to a twig or leaf stem, using silk, and slips off its last caterpillar skin to reveal a chrysalis.

Most moths and butterflies make silk, which is produced in short lengths by their salivary glands. The caterpillar glues these threads together to make a cocoon

MOST BUTTERFLIES AND MOTHS DON'T EAT FOOD, BUT JUST DRINK TO SURVIVE.

to protect itself during the chrysalis stage. The ermine moth builds a lacy net container, the moon moth a chrysalis with a silver sheen.

From the outside, a chrysalis looks lifeless, a dead thing hanging from a branch. But inside something amazing happens. Part of the caterpillar dies, but other tiny cell clusters grow. Slowly the growing cells form a new body. One day the cocoon splits, a head with two huge eyes appears, then legs, and finally a butterfly or moth crawls into the world.

Moths and Butterflies

If you see a moth in the daytime, it is most probably a butterfly! Generally moths fly by night, butterflies by day. Butterflies are brightly colored, while moths' colorings tend to be duller. When a butterfly rests, it holds its wings upright over its body, but a moth spreads its wings out or folds them over its back. If you get close enough to see, a moth's antennae are feathered or pointed, while a butterfly's are club-tipped.

ANT AND THE BUTTERFLY

An ant, running in the sunshine, came across a chrysalis that was near its time of change. The ant looked at the dry, shrivelled cocoon and scoffed. It boasted how it could run where it wanted, climb a tree if it wished, while the chrysalis could only lay imprisoned in its shell, unable to do anything. A few hours later, the ant passed that way again, and found only an empty shell where the chrysalis had been. Suddenly the ant felt a cool breeze and there above him, fanning its wings, was a beautiful butterfly. "You can boast to me as much as you like now," said the butterfly, and flew away leaving the ant far behind.

A newly hatched butterfly spreads its wings out in the Sun to dry before it flies off.

Moths' wings usually blend in perfectly with the habitat in which they live, making them difficult to see.

Beetles

Beetles have long been viewed with superstition. The scarab, or dung beetle, was sacred to the ancient Egyptians and was often carved on seal stones or amulets. The scarab takes fresh dung, rolls it into a ball with his front and back legs, and then trundles it backward until he comes to a spot where he digs a hole and buries the dung. The female then lays her eggs inside. Because the ball was the same shape as the Sun, and the beetle moved its ball like the Sun moves across the sky, the Egyptians adopted the beetle as a symbol of life and resurrection.

Jumping Fleas

A flea can jump 130 times his own height—that's the same as a human jumping to the top of a 70-storey building! To achieve these incredible leaps, fleas have to accelerate with a force 20 times greater than the force required to launch a space rocket. They can also jump 350 times their own body length: that's like a human jumping the length of a football field.

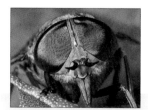

Flies' Eyes

Like all insects, flies have compound eyes: eyes that consist of numerous separate light-sensitive units. Each unit has its own lens, so flies and other insects see objects as a mosaic of overlapping points of light. Flies cannot focus sharply on objects, but pick up the slightest movements around them.

Insects

AT LEAST THREE-QUARTERS of the known animal species are insects—that's more than one million for every person on Earth. Insects were the first creatures to fly. The earliest known insects had two pairs of wings that did not fold, and could be flapped alternately, much like dragonflies today. The bodies of insects vary greatly in size, from less than $1/100$ in (0.25 mm) to 10 in (25 cm,) and in shape, but they all have a head, thorax, and an abdomen.

NOT ALL INSECTS FLY. An acre of pasture land contains around 360 million insects, most of which are wingless, leaping insects.

The thorax of an insect is divided into three parts, each of which has a pair of legs. Insects breathe through their abdomens by means of tiny air holes which lead into tubes, called "trachea," along which air travels around the insect's body. Insects eat in two ways: by sucking or chewing. If they have jaw-like "mandibles"

THE FIRE BEETLE OF AUSTRALIA CAN WALK THROUGH RED-HOT ASHES.

then they chew their food, if they have tube-like "proboscis," like a butterfly, they suck their food.

Flies can walk on almost every surface, even upside down on the ceiling. This is because each of their feet have a pair of hooks and two pads covered with tiny hairs that are sticky at the ends. But they don't just use their feet for walking. Blowflies can taste sugar through their feet, which are covered with sweet-sensitive

taste-buds—they can taste traces of sugar millions of times more efficiently than the human tongue. Ichneumon flies can even hear and smell through their feet. Mayflies do not eat their whole life long as they don't have a mouth, but they only live for two to five hours, at the most, a few days. The crane fly is so allergic to warmth that the touch of a human hand may kill it.

The dragonfly is the state insect of Alaska, and was chosen to represent the area, because,

SOME TINY MIDGES BEAT THEIR WINGS 50,000 TIMES A MINUTE.

according to the Governor of Alaska, "the dragonfly's ability to hover and fly forward and backward reminds us of the skillful maneuvring of the bush pilots in Alaska." In fact, a dragonfly can outdo any pilot as it can stop dead at 35 mph (56 kph,) fly backward, and

Ladybugs have two sets of wings, a hard outer pair that protect a soft inner pair.

FLIGHT MUSCLES WORK WELL IN WARM CONDITIONS—SOME INSECTS CAN'T FLY IF IT'S TOO COLD.

make very sudden turns. Like all flies, dragonflies have compound eyes and can spot food 120 ft (37 m) away. They fly with their legs together to form baskets in which to capture insects that they eat while still in the air.

The skeletons of insects are on the outside of their bodies, and other body bits are often in unexpected places. A locust's ear is in his abdomen, while a daddy long-leg's ears are in his feet.

HOVERFLIES HAVE STABILIZERS BEHIND THEIR WINGS SO THEY CAN HOVER PERFECTLY STILL.

Dragonflies are one of the few insects that have not changed much since prehistoric times.

Ladybugs

There are male and female ladybugs. Underneath their hard outer wings, they have paper-thin flying wings that they flap nearly 100 times a second as they fly. Ladybugs eat aphids and other plant-harming insects. One story says that in the Middle Ages, plagues of insects were eating the crops. The people prayed to Mary for help, and a swarm of ladybugs came and ate the pests, so they called the little bug "beetle of Our Lady."

Little Leapers

There are more than 20,000 kinds of grasshoppers and crickets. The chirping sound they make is produced by the rubbing together of the rigid veins on their front wings, or by rubbing part of the back leg against the wing vein. If you want to know how hot it is, count the number of chirps a cricket makes in fourteen seconds, add forty, and the result is the temperature in Fahrenheit.

River Fly

A legend from eastern Canada tells how, when the world was new, there was a beautiful river. Fish swam in it, beavers built lodges in it, and all the animals came to drink there. Then a great moose came along and began to drink the river dry. Everyone was worried, but nothing they said or did persuaded him to go away. Then the fly promised to get rid of the giant moose. The animals laughed, "You! You're so tiny!" Fly said nothing, but when the moose appeared he landed on the moose's nose and bit it sharply. Then he jumped all over the moose, biting and biting, until eventually the moose could stand no more and ran away.

Owls

Owl Eyes

Owls have huge eyes that can hold a fixed stare. They have a third eyelid, which moves from side to side to clean their eyes and clear their vision. An owl's pupils can contract or expand quickly to adapt to light conditions, but its eyes are fixed in one position, so it must turn its whole head to look around. One of an owl's eyes is set higher than the other. This helps it to judge accurately how far away an object is.

Pellets

Owls eat the whole of their prey, so much of what they eat cannot be broken down by their digestive system. An owl regurgitates this part of its meal, but first the bones, hair, and feathers are all squashed together to form pellets. By examining owl pellets, naturalists can discover what owls eat.

B ECAUSE IT CAN SEE in the dark and looks thoughtful and serious, in ancient cultures the owl was taken as a symbol of wisdom, seeing through the darkness of ignorance. In modern western culture, the owl is also linked with ghosts and dark forces. This is probably because most owls fly mainly at night, flitting about silently, and letting out occasional mournful hoots.

OWLS ARE SHORT-tailed, soft-feathered birds with big heads and enormous eyes. Their beaks are hooked and partially hidden by feathers.

Lords of the night, most owls hunt after dark. With eyesight a hundred times sharper than ours, an owl can see through the

MOST OWLS CAN HEAR SOUNDS TEN TIMES SOFTER THAN A HUMAN EAR.

leaves and overhanging branches to the forest floor, where mice and voles scamper about. As soon as owls see the tiniest movement below, they swoop down and grab the small creature in their claws, killing it with their sharp-hooked talons.

Owls come in all shapes and sizes, from one that is so small it lives inside a desert cactus, to the great horned owl, which is the only bird of prey that can outfly

OWLS' WINGS ARE FRINGED WITH SOFT FEATHERS TO MAKE THEIR FLIGHTS ALMOST SILENT.

The barred owl makes its home in swamps and dense woods, while the burrowing owl gets its name because it either digs its own burrow or takes over the abandoned tunnel of a prairie dog.

The eastern screech owl is also called the "shivering owl" and the great horned owl, a fierce hunter, has been nicknamed the "tiger of the night."

Among the larger species of owls are the eagle owls, that look

THE ELF OWL, AT ONLY 6 IN (15 CM) LONG, IS ONE OF THE SMALLEST OWLS IN THE WORLD.

as if they have pointed ears sticking up on the tops of their heads. These are just tufts of feathers and are not connected to their hearing at all. The northern hawk owl, found mainly in Canada, North America, Northern Asia, and Scandinavia, deviates from owl rules as it is the only owl to hunt by day rather than by night. In flight it looks a little like a hawk, with its short pointed wings and an unusually long tail.

When hunting, a barn owl flies 6¹/₂–13 ft (2–4 m) above the ground.

the golden eagle. The snowy owl lives in the tundra regions of the Arctic and has a wing-span of about 5 ft (1.5 m) and often hunts during the day.

Owl Ears

Roger Payne, a student at Cornell University, U.S., placed an owl in a large wooden shed. The shed was sealed, so no light could enter and the floor was covered in dry leaves. In pitch darkness, Payne released a live mouse. As soon as the mouse rustled in the leaves, the owl left its perch. Payne snapped on the light just in time to see the owl with the mouse in its talons. When Payne plugged one of the owl's ears, the owl was unable to find the prey in the dark.

Twit-Twoo

The owl's hoot has many superstitions attached to it. An Old English belief was that the screech owl only called when rain was on the way. In some areas of rural France it is thought that if a pregnant woman hears an owl hoot, she will have a baby girl. In ancient Rome and in Celtic lore an owl that hooted at the time of death was believed to be waiting for the soul of the dying person. In ancient Rome, the owl evidently appeared at the deathbeds of several emperors and the death of Dido was foretold by an owl alighting on her house.

SWIFT AND SILENT

One report tells the story of a man who loved owls. Every morning he fed a wild great gray owl that had a wingspan of around 5 ft (1.5 m.) One morning the man was outside collecting stones to put in a tank with some frogs. He picked up three gray stones and was holding them in the palm of his hand, when suddenly, they were not there anymore. All he had in his hand was a bright red gash, oozing blood. Faster than he could blink, and more silently than he could imagine, the owl had swooped down, grabbed the stones, and was already sitting on a branch about 6¹/₂ ft (2 m) away.

Storks

ODDITIES OF THE bird world, the stork, with its white feathers, long legs, and strange walk has been the source of many superstitions. In western countries, the white stork is said to bring new babies to parents. This legend may have begun because storks are seen in and around water, and water is traditionally associated with fertility. It may simply be because storks take good care of their young.

Mother Love

Once, a thatched roof on which a stork was nesting caught fire. The stork sat over its young to protect them and beat at the flames with its wings. When the fire was extinguished, the stork was black with soot and smoke burns, but at least its children were safe. Mother storks are very protective animals. On hot days, they have been seen carrying water in their bills to give their young a drink.

Storks are gregarious birds and don't mind living alongside humans.

STORKS ARE LARGE, long-legged wading birds, with elongated necks, long broad wings, and webbed feet. They are strong

THERE ARE 17 SPECIES OF STORK LIVING THROUGHOUT THE WORLD.

fliers and look particularly striking in flight with their necks and legs stretched out, legs hanging down slightly. When members of a breeding pair meet they perform a greeting ceremony by clattering their bills. They feed mostly on frogs, reptiles, insects, and mollusks. White storks live in Europe and western Asia during the summer and migrate south to Africa in the winter. They often nest on top of trees or houses. Once a nest is made, it is used and added to year after year. Over the years a nest can grow into a cylinder of twigs 6 ft (1.8 m) high and 4 ft (1.2 m) wide. In the nest, the female lays

THE OPENBILL STORK HAS A GAP BETWEEN ITS BILL, WHICH ONLY MEETS AT THE TIP.

between one and five eggs, which both parents incubate.

Cranes

CRANES ARE large, graceful birds that can be found on five of the world's seven continents. South America and Antarctica are the only places they do not inhabit. Cranes are one of the most threatened bird species, and of the 15 types, 11 are in danger of becoming extinct.

SPLENDID-LOOKING, with brightly-colored bare skin on their faces and decorative plumes on their heads, cranes are aggressive birds. When a crane is fighting another crane, it leaps into the air to stab at its opponent with its bill or rakes it with sharp claws. The fighting continues until one bird flies or runs away, sometimes closely pursued by the victor. A running crane takes one to three steps per second, and may use its wings for balance and speed. Cranes can easily outrun humans.

Eurasion cranes and sandhill

THE LARGER SPECIES OF CRANE STAND AT 5 FT (1.5 M) TALL.

cranes prepare themselves for the breeding season. They preen mud into their feathers, and, in the case of the Siberian crane, on their necks too. This helps to camouflage them in the marsh lands, but it also helps them to attract a mate.

Cranes are good swimmers, although they do not have webbed feet. Chicks follow their parents into the water within hours of hatching. A chick in distress calls for its parents in a high-pitched peep, while adults call to each other with a soft purring.

After breeding, cranes fly in large flocks in V-formation or in line to warmer southern climates.

Crane Dance

Cranes migrate in the winter. In the spring, when they return, they perform a wonderful mating dance. Hornborgar Lake in Sweden has become a tourist attraction as people flock there each spring to see around 70,000 cranes dancing. In some countries, traditional dancers copy the movements of the crane and add them to their dances.

Whooping Crane

The cry of the whooping crane sounds like an Indian war cry. The world's population of whooping cranes is less than 250, and they are in danger of disappearing altogether. Their one breeding area is in Wood Buffalo National Park in Canada. Cranes like privacy, and although in 1943, Robert Parker Allen was appointed to protect and conserve whooping cranes, it was not until 1955 that he and his team actually found where the cranes were hiding.

KUNG FU

The art of Kung Fu is an ancient Tibetan form of self-defense, which uses quick body movements to evade and retaliate at the same time. Many years ago, an old man was sitting by a pond, thinking and watching a crane, when a gorilla came out of the forest and attacked the bird. The old man was sure the crane would be killed, but was amazed at how the crane avoided and defeated the ape. Cranes dodge about to confuse an attacker, and gracefully use their wings to parry blows and sometimes catch an attacker's blow at an angle that throws it off balance. They also use their claws as weapons. The "White Crane" style of Kung Fu imitates these actions.

Two-headed Eagle

Some countries have used the symbol of a two-headed eagle to show they are all-powerful and are watching everywhere. The Hittites carved it on their monuments, then it appeared in Byzantium, and later, in 1155, Frederick Barbarossa, king of the Romans, chose it as a symbol for the Holy Roman Empire. Finally it was adopted by Ivan III of Russia in 1472.

Legions of the Eagle

Ancient Persians and Romans going into battle carried eagle standards as symbols of their power and bravery. Every French regiment in Napoleon's army carried a bronze standard in the form of an eagle. Eagles were painted onto many shields during the Crusades and they are also one of the many emblems of chivalry.

Fancy Feathers

Eagle feathers are used around the world on clothing, ceremonial tools, and head-dresses. In Native American lore, a head-dress made from eagle feathers symbolizes the Thunderbird, the Great Spirit, and the feathers carry the prayers of the tribe up to the sky.

Eagles

EAGLES NEST and fly higher than any other birds, and so were thought to converse with the gods. They have entered our hearts and our imaginations as creatures of power, inspiring awe and a longing that we too could fly to the realms of the gods. Often seen as king of birds, this bird of prey has always been a symbol of royalty, authority, strength, victory, and pride.

ALTHOUGH NOT THE swiftest of birds, the eagle has captured human imagination. His wings are an engineering marvel, not only powerful enough to carry him high and far, but have feathers that act like wind-flaps to increase lift, reduce turbulence, and prevent stalling at low speeds. When an eagle spirals upward toward the Sun, he is in fact coasting downhill on rising air.

AN EAGLE'S EYESIGHT IS EIGHT TIMES MORE POWERFUL THAN A HUMAN'S.

He rises because the upward-moving air is traveling faster upward than it is traveling downward, rather like someone walking down an upward-moving escalator. His wings are not designed for speed, but for soaring.

There are 59 species of eagles around the world. Groups of bald eagles gather by rivers near the

EAGLETS (YOUNG EAGLES) HAVE TO BE TAUGHT HOW TO HUNT AND KILL.

Alaskan coast, where they prey on fish. Bald eagles breed in northern North America on inland lakes, and sometimes migrate in the south to find food. Pairs stay together year to year, and engage in elaborate courtship displays by locking talons mid-air and somersaulting down together. They make their nests of sticks in large trees or on rocks, and add to it year after year.

One of the largest eagles in the world is the golden eagle, which measures about 3 ft (90 cm) from the tip of his beak to the tip of his tail, and has a wingspan of about

The bald eagle is far from featherless, but has a lighter cap that covers his head.

7 ft (2 m.) When hunting, the golden eagle soars for long periods, using his incredibly sharp eyesight to scan the countryside, then diving down to seize an animal. He uses his powerful back talon to kill the prey, while his front three grip the animal securely.

EAGLES KILL WITH THEIR CLAWS AND USE THEIR SHARP BEAKS TO CUT THROUGH FLESH.

Despite the power of his beak and talons, and the fierceness of his eye, the eagle has a very weak voice that is almost a chirp. Golden eagles build large, untidy nests in tall trees or on rocky ledges and these can be 6 ft (1.8 m) in diameter.

Like eagles, vultures are birds of prey too, but they scavenge the left-overs of other animals.

Bald Eagle

The bald eagle was adopted by the U.S. in 1782 as the national emblem. It appears on coins and paper money, and is symbolic of power and strength. In the emblem, the eagle's wings are outstretched to show his power, but his foot rests on an olive branch to show that power is sheathed in peace. The bald eagle is not bald, but has a white head. The word "bald" comes from the old English "balde" which means "white."

EAGLE SNATCHER

One tale tells of a woman whose baby was snatched by an eagle. The baby had been wrapped in a shawl and laid to sleep in a corner of a harvest field, where his mother was working. The eagle, which was nested high on a nearby cliff, could be clearly seen flying back home with the baby in his mouth. The cliff was very steep and no one had climbed it before, but the desperate mother ran after the bird and somehow managed to climb up to the nest. In it she found the baby, alive and unharmed, still wrapped in the shawl. She snatched the baby from under the eagle's beak, and climbed shakily back down the cliff.

Parrots

BRIGHTLY COLORED tree-living birds, parrots have fascinated us for as long as we have had contact with them. Their colorful plumage, and engaging behavior, makes them one of nature's great attractions. From the largest macaw, to the tiniest budgie, members of the parrot family are known as hookbills because of their short, powerful, and strongly-hooked beaks.

Scarlet macaws fly off noisily at the slightest disturbance.

Talking Birds

Parrots can talk. Until recently it was thought that their "speech" was just sound mimicry, but more recent research has shown they can interpret some of what is said to them and they can learn spoken phrases and identify symbols. Dr. Irene Pepperberg of the University of Arizona, U.S. works with African gray parrots. Alex, the oldest parrot, can identify five shapes, seven colors, and over one hundred objects. It also knows many phrases and when to use them.

PARROTS ARE found over the warmer parts of the world, from the rain forest regions of America and Africa, to Australia, New Guinea, and the Solomon Islands. In the wild they are graceful birds. Macaws are among the most beautiful and flamboyant of the parrots. At home in the rain forests and savanna of South and Central America, they are seen less and less in the wild because of the destruction of their natural habitat, and because so many of these birds are caught to be sold as pets. Macaws form strong pair bonds, and in the spring every adult screams for a partner. They nest in holes in trees, and as they make their daily trips to the feeding grounds, pairs fly together, wings almost touching.

AS PARROTS CLIMB UP TREES THEY USE THEIR CURVED BEAKS AS WELL AS THEIR CLAWS.

Parakeets are fairly small, sociable parrots. They are extremely noisy and are usually seen in small flocks, although they may gather in their hundreds at feeding sites. Seeds, berries, fruit, flowers, and nectar are their usual food. Monk parakeets build nests at the beginning of the breeding season. At first they have only a few compartments, but are gradually added to until there are up to 20, each inhabited by a pair of birds.

PARROTS CAN LIVE FOR BETWEEN 50 AND 70 YEARS.

Toucans

AMONG THE MOST extraordinary birds in the world, toucans live in the dense rain forests of the Amazon region and South America. A toucan's boldly colored beak makes up almost half of its body length, and its plumage is usually dark, with contrasting color on its head and neck.

PROBABLY THE MOST well-known toucan is the large toco toucan. Toco's plumage is mainly black and white with a few red tail-feathers. Its golden bill is about $7^1/_2$ in (9 cm) long and you might think it would overbalance when flying, but the bill is lighter than it looks. Like all toucans, it feeds on fruit, and has a great liking for passion fruit and peppers. Tocos are not at all shy and will come

THE SHY EMERALD TOUCANET LIVES AT AN ALTITUDE OF UP TO 10,000 FT (3,000 M.)

into houses and steal food if given the chance.

Toucans nest in holes in trees either made naturally or abandoned by woodpeckers. If a hole is not big enough, a toucan enlarges it by pecking away at the trunk with its beak, letting the wood chips fall to the ground to make a soft base. Its nest is usually about 12–24 in (30–61 cm) deep to make room for its large beak.

A female toucan lays two to four eggs, which are incubated by both parents. After 15 days

A TOUCAN'S TONGUE IS NARROW WITH BRISTLES AT THE TIP AND LOOKS LIKE A FEATHER.

the chicks hatch, but they are naked and blind until they are about three weeks old.

Snappy Eater

If you have ever tried throwing peanuts or sweets up into the air and catching them in your mouth, then you have been imitating a toucan. A toucan seizes its food with the tip of its bill, throws its head back, and tosses the item into its mouth. Toucans enjoy playing with their food in the wild and often toss it high into the air and then fly up to catch it!

The toco toucan lives in small groups and likes to visit coconut and sugar plantations.

All Sorts

There are 42 kinds of toucan, ranging from birds 13 in (33 cm) to birds 25 in (63.5 cm) long. Although they all have large bills, these differ in size and style from species to species. The curl-crested aracari has jagged notches on its blue-striped beak. The plate-billed mountain toucanet has a horny yellow plate that grows from each side of its upper bill, while the emerald toucanet has yellow and black stripes along the length of its bill.

TOP OF THE BILL

Toucans eat mainly soft food, such as small fruits, although their bills are hard enough to dig into tree trunks in search of insects. Their remarkable beaks are constructed of a light, horn-like material called keratin. Inside, the bills are hollow and honey-combed with a network of struts, which keeps them light for flying but also gives them strength. The beaks have sawlike edges, which enable the birds to tear off large pieces of fruit. The reasons for such a large beak are not clearly understood. However, toucans sometimes use their bills to "fence" with each other in play, and the brilliant yellow color is probably used to attract mates.

Pigeons

DOVES AND PIGEONS belong to the same family of birds. Descended from the wild rock dove, they have been domesticated for centuries. The ancient Egyptians kept them as long ago as 3000 B.C. Although all originally from one species, years of selective breeding have produced many types and sizes of domestic pigeon.

MANY VARIETIES OF WILD pigeons and doves can be found in all parts of the world except very cold regions. If you walk in woodlands, you might hear the cooing of pigeons, or be startled by the loud flapping of their wings as they leave their nests. The wood pigeon and stock dove make their nests in trees or holes in trees, while the rock dove nests in holes in the cliffs of wild, rocky coasts.

If they are not using holes to nest in, pigeons and doves build little rafts

THE PASSENGER PIGEON WAS HUNTED TO EXTINCTION IN THE 1800S.

of twigs and sticks, with a slight hollow in the center for their eggs. Pigeons usually lay two eggs at a time, and newly hatched pigeons are strange-looking little creatures. Blind and helpless, they have bluish-black skin with no feathers, just a few tufts of yellow down. The parents feed the young birds with a curdlike white "milk" from a part of their throats called the

Some people place dovecotes in their gardens as houses for pigeons.

Symbol of Peace

The dove has been seen as a sacred bird and a symbol of peace since ancient times. It is the one creature into which neither the Devil nor a witch can change themselves. To Christians the dove is a symbol of the "Holy Spirit." In Roman mythology it was thought to be the messenger of Venus, the goddess of love.

Final Tribute

During his life, Captain Joseph Belain of the U.S. Navy spent a great deal of time and effort working to save the carrier pigeon service from falling into disuse. When he died, his burial service was held in the church of Gay Head, U.S. During the service a carrier pigeon flew in from the sea and sat on the coffin until it was over.

Dove Tail

Each pigeon wing contains 20 flight feathers. When they are spread, the feathers overlap each other without any gaps. In the ancient Greek myth of Jason and the Argonauts, Jason was rowing across the sea when he came to a narrow channel. The only way through was to navigate between the "Symplegades"—clashing rocks that moved around in the sea, crushing ships as they passed through. Jason released a dove, which flew through the channel, losing only its tail feathers as the rocks crashed together. This enabled Jason to judge the time it would take for him to row through the passage.

crop. When pigeons first leave their nests at around 23 days old, they can't fly.

Pigeons are a familiar sight in city squares the world over. Perhaps the most closely linked to humans are the carrier pigeons.

PIGEONS ARE THE ONLY BIRDS THAT CAN SUCK—OTHER BIRDS JUST SIP AND SWALLOW.

Pigeons have a strong instinct to fly home to the place where they roost or were bred, and have an ability to do this over a long distance. They navigate using various information sources, such as the Earth's magnetic field, movement of the Sun and stars, wind direction, and cloud movements. Because of these homing instincts, pigeons are ideal messengers and for most of our history, they have been able to fly faster and more directly than any other means of transport. Carrier pigeons can fly at speeds of 30-60 mph (48–97 kph.)

Pigeons were used as messengers during World War I and II. It was a Japanese officer who first noticed that all Chinese sailing ships had pigeons aboard,

THE FIRST PIGEON POST WAS STARTED IN A.D. 1150 BY THE SULTAN OF BAGHDAD.

and that if the birds were released in the morning, they always returned to the ship at night. The officer experimented by releasing racing birds from mobile lofts, and found that the pigeons returned to the lofts wherever they were.

Pigeons are naturally afraid of the loud noise of gunfire, so the fact that so many of them flew through artillery, shrapnel, and

machine-gun fire, as well as through gas, fog, and rain to deliver messages is quite amazing.

In World War II, the British army dropped boxes of homing pigeons by parachute behind enemy lines. They were used by resistance fighters to send messages back to London, U.K.

Racing pigeons are also popular. In Belgium their flying abilities form the basis for a national sport. A racing pigeon can fly at around 60 mph (97 kph) or even more with a following wind. Different types of birds are used for different distances. Light birds are sprinters—they can fly fast in short bursts, but the larger ones are used for long-distance flight. Under good conditions pigeons can fly for 13 hours non-stop.

Carrier pigeons are homing pigeons. They have excellent navigational skills and return home after delivering messages.

Red Feet

An Arabian legend tells the tale of how the pigeon got its red feet. After the world was flooded, Noah released the dove from the Ark. When it returned with an olive branch in its beak, Noah knew the tree tops were appearing and the floods receding. Noah released the bird for a second time and again it returned, but with red mud on its feet. This showed that the dove had been able to land on dry ground. Noah asked God if the dove's feet could forever be red to remind humankind of the time the world flooded.

LOYAL PIGEON

In 1939, Hugh Perkins, the son of the sheriff of Summersville, West Virginia, U.S., took in a stray carrier pigeon. He gave the bird the number 167. In April 1940, Perkins was taken seriously ill and had to be rushed to the nearest hospital, which was at Philippi, 100 miles (161 km) away. One night in the hospital, there was a tapping at the ward window. When the nurse drew back the curtain, there was a carrier pigeon, tapping its beak on the pane. "Let it in," said Hugh, "I bet it's mine. See if the number 167 is on its leg." The nurse opened the window and the bird flew in and perched on Hugh's bed. When he checked, the number was 167!

Crows and ravens

CROWS AND RAVENS belong to the same family and are among the most intelligent of the birds. They have amazing memories, are good at solving puzzles, and like and collect shiny objects. They are adaptable birds and are good opportunists that can change their habits according to the new situations in which they find themselves.

Birds of Ill Omen

Large black birds have often been linked to the devil in folklore, and are seen as omens of death or bad luck. To the Romans, the raven's cry of "cras, cras" meant "tomorrow, tomorrow" and so was a symbol of hope. To the Christians ravens were an emblem of God's providing, because ravens fed the prophet Elijah. Saints were often drawn with ravens beside them.

Ravens in the Tower

The raven is supposed to be able to see into the future, and to smell death from a distance. There are always ravens at the Tower of London, in the U.K., supposedly to protect Britain against invasion. Legend has it that if the ravens leave the Tower, Britain will fall to an enemy.

RAVENS ARE ABOUT a third larger than crows, with a heavier bill, which is long and slightly hooked. They have more fan-shaped tails than crows, and their plumage has a bluish, satiny sheen. Sometimes ravens have a ruff of feathers around the throat. They spend the winter in flocks, but nest

CROWS EAT INSECTS, SPIDERS, FROGS, AND SMALL MAMMALS, BUT ALSO SCAVENGE ON REFUSE.

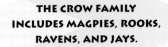

THE CROW FAMILY INCLUDES MAGPIES, ROOKS, RAVENS, AND JAYS.

alone in tall trees or on cliff faces.

The carrion crow is about 19 in (47 cm) in length and its plumage is all black. Hooded crows with their gray body and black head, wings, and tail, are a distinct species of the crow family.

Rooks are slightly smaller than crows, and have a longer, thinner beak with a bare patch of skin between the eyes, and shaggy, loose feathers on the thighs. They are more social than crows and if you see a flock of birds near a colony of untidy nests in a group of trees, then they will be rooks, not crows. Rooks are useful to farmers, because they eat insects and worms that damage crop roots.

A GROUP OF RAVENS IS CALLED A MURDER.

Crows and rooks seem to be interested in watching how other animals behave. They sometimes tease or annoy other creatures by pecking them or pulling their tails. They have learned that by doing this, they can distract an animal long enough to steal its food. Crows and ravens are also good at imitating sounds, and have been known to copy words. Ravens can imitate other birds, falling water, and even mimic music. Jim Nollman, an author, naturalist, and pioneer in the field of interspecies communications, tells of a raven that joined him

Crows can move fast on the ground as well as in the air.

on a camping trip. For an hour or more, the raven sat beside him while Nollman played a Jew's harp, the raven contentedly croaking a low imitation of the

ROOKS' NESTS

Strict rules apply in a rookery, and if younger birds try to build a nest some distance away from the main rookery, older birds will destroy it. It has also long been legend that rooks have "parliaments" where judgements are passed. One lady wrote of seeing a pair of young rooks build a nest in a tree farther along her driveway from the rookery trees. Three times the older rooks destroyed it and three times the younger rooks rebuilt it. One day the disobedient pair were encircled and flown to a nearby meadow. After much cawing, the mass of rooks rose in the air, and started to peck the culprits as a punishment.

TAME ROOKS CAN LEARN TO IMITATE HUMAN SPEECH.

sound, like a slowed up version of a cat purring.

The Clark's nutcracker of North America, a member of the crow family, buries pine cones as food stores, and can remember up to 3,000 individual places it has buried them. Ravens don't like people to see them hide food. If they think they are being watched they dig it up and hide it again.

During the nesting season rooks gather in large communal roosts, called rookeries to breed.

Raven Fortune-teller

The raven is seen as a shapeshifter and an omen of change. In Norse mythology, the god Odin relied on two ravens for news of what was happening in the world. They sat, one on each shoulder, and were called Huginn and Muninn (Mind and Memory.) In days of old, the magical emblem of the Danish standard was the "Fatal Raven." Its wings would move to forecast the results of a battle: if they hung by its side, the Danes would be defeated, but if it spread, then victory was certain.

Animal symbols

IN EVERY SOCIETY, animals have been and still are used as symbols. Sometimes they represent different character traits, such as: "eager as a beaver," "sly as a fox," or "dead as a dodo." At other times animals are symbols of inspiration—the Romans used the eagle on their military standards as a sign of great honor. Looking at animals and their abilities can help us to understand things about ourselves that need to be changed or developed.

Proud as a Peacock

This saying came from the fact that a peacock's feathers are extremely beautiful and the animal is often seen showing them off.

Totem poles

Native Americans carved totem poles to tell a story. Each house had its own pole outside, which showed who lived there and how they ranked in society. You could say that the animals on the totem pole symbolized the tribe in the same way as a flag symbolizes a nation. Birds and animals were also carved on the poles to represent the different behaviors, powers, and skills for which people hoped. A *potlatch* was a ceremonial feast and traditionally new poles were raised at these feasts to honor a *potlatch* host, or sometimes depict a tribal legend. Here are some well-known totem pole animals and what they represent:

- Horses—loyalty
- Hummingbirds—joy
- Deer—gentleness
- Hawks—communication
- Buffalo—abundance

Power animals

Native Americans and other cultures believed that the whole of creation is linked and dependent on each other: humans, animals, birds, and nature, and that to be balanced as people we need to relate properly to all of creation. Every living thing has something to teach us if we study it closely. In many societies people chose, or were given, "power animals" —animals whose characters and strengths symbolized their own traits, or those which they wished to develop. Each person had between two and nine power animals. When they called on the power of an animal, they tried to understand that animal and to learn something from it. For example, if a wolf was the chosen power animal, they would be a teacher or leader, someone whose instinct was linked with intelligence.

Other wolf animal traits are that they value their family, are loyal, and are good at protecting themselves.

How to find your power animals

The animals, birds, or other creatures to which you are drawn, or which you fear are most likely to be those that have lessons to teach you. Answer the following questions, then look at some of the other power animals we have picked out below, and see if any of them are for you:

1) Of all the animals in the world, which are you most interested in?
2) If you go to a zoo, which animal do you want to see first?
3) Do some animals constantly seem to "appear" in your life?
4) Which animals frighten you? Sometimes we need to come to understand what we fear for the fear to go away and for power to take its place.
5) Do you have dreams of certain animals, or of one particular animal?
6) Do you collect any animal ornaments or draw pictures of animals?
7) Do you have pictures of one particular animal on your bedroom wall?
8) Do people say that you remind them of a certain animal?
9) Which animal do you most admire?

Giraffes

stretch to reach new heights of achievement
•
look at things in a new way
•
learn to use their inner vision—act on instinct
•
think ahead when doing or planning something

Kangaroos

jump away from bad situations
•
value a safe home
•
protect those weaker
•
are adaptable to new situations

Skunks

have self-respect
•
have courage
•
are self-confident
•
are in touch with their own energy flow

Lizards

face their fears
•
learn how to control their dreams
•
learn that they can heal themselves
•
aren't too self-important

Black Rhinos

learn to be happy with their own company
•
get to know themselves
•
trust their instincts
•
learn more about ancient wisdom and how to use it

Tasmanian Devils

are able to defend themselves
•
protect their own space and stand up for their rights
•
have the wisdom to know when it is right to fight for a cause and what to fight for

Snails

understand the value of leaving a mark in life
•
think that to slow down is sometimes a good thing
•
know that sometimes retreat is the best form of defense
•
keep going and trying, even if each step forward is a small one

Seagulls

learn to detach from problems and see them "from above"
•
are friends to others
•
behave responsibly
•
tune into energies that they cannot see, but which are around them

Animal spirit

Our main power animals never leave, but walk either side of us throughout life to guard and guide us. If you have a number of animals that come to mind, think hard about which one draws you most. One may well be your "within" animal who teaches you how to be true to yourself and find your heart's joy.

More and more people are awakening to the idea that our bodies, minds, and spirits are one: that what we think and how we feel has a real affect on our bodies. In the same way, the physical world and the world of spirit affect each other. When we refuse to listen to our spirit, our deepest inner self, we stop being who we really could be.

Creature dreams

DREAMS ARE MESSAGES from our subconscious mind, and the images in our dreams usually symbolize our worries and concerns. Often animals feature in our dreams. They may represent our strengths and weaknesses, or serve to highlight aspects of a problem we are dealing with in our waking lives. For example, dreaming of a lion blocking your path may mean that you are facing something that is difficult for you cope with.

Animal dreamers

Scientists tell us that it is possible to tell when a sleeper is dreaming by monitoring the REM (rapid eye movement.) The REM of sleeping animals has also been monitored and it has been proven that prey animals, like stags, dream less than hunters, like tigers. Both cats and dogs twitch and mutter when dreaming.

Our dreams are individual to us and form part of who we are.

How to remember your dreams

Whether we remember or not, we all dream a few times each night. If you don't remember your dreams easily, you can program yourself to recall them in the following ways:

1) Say to yourself, three times, before you go to sleep, "I will remember my dreams."

2) Keep a notebook and pencil beside your bed and write down all you can remember of your dream as soon as you awake. If you do this for a few weeks, the dreams may form a pattern.

3) If you wake with a dream in your head and as soon as you move it fades, turn immediately back to the position you were in when you awoke, and the dream may come back.

Only you can interpret your dreams because dream messages come to us in symbols and your mind will have its own symbols. Below are some animals and some information on how to interpret them when they appear in your dreams.

Animals form such a large part of our waking life it is no surprise they feature so predominantly in our dreams.

Baboon

If you dream about a baboon something good may be coming your way. For a young woman it means she will soon make a happy marriage. Generally, baboons indicate good luck and success in your life and maybe an improvement in status. They are also a good sign for a business venture.

Birds

Birds bring mixed messages. Dead or injured birds foretell worries unless they are birds of prey, in which case they show that any worries you may have will soon be over. Singing, flying, or brightly colored birds are all signs of good fortune.

Adder

This poisonous snake can be a sign that you have friends who are not true friends. It can also indicate a family row or embarrassment because you have been deceitful. If you kill an adder, it can mean that you triumph over an enemy.

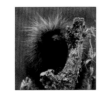

Porcupine

Dreaming of a porcupine could mean that a person will come into your life who you would like to know better, but who you find it difficult to get close to. It may indicate that good things are on their way, but you will have a difficult time just before they arrive.

Fish

Because fish swim in water and water has always symbolized emotions, fish represent messages from your emotions. They may signify that you need to look at what you are really feeling in your life just now.

Frog

Dreaming of frogs is a good omen because they bring friendship and personal happiness. To hear them croaking means everything will go well in your life at home and in the community. Frogs can also be a sign of restfulness and contentment, and are symbols of sincere friends who love and understand you.

Kangaroo

To see a kangaroo with a baby in its pouch means that you will go on an unexpected trip. Dreaming of a jumping kangaroo foretells an aeroplane journey. If the kangaroo is female the journey will be full of adventure. Fighting kangaroos mean you can expect setbacks.

Animals and religion

MANY RELIGIONS GREW from an attempt to explain what we could not understand —to solve the riddles of who we are and why we are here, and to answer the questions of where we came from and where we go on to. Animals were often used as symbols to represent an aspect of reality or belief, and were worshiped as gods themselves. In some cultures the animal was kept in the temple of the god, and when it died, was buried during a special ceremony.

Eagles

Most cultures that have gods of the sky worship the eagle in some way. To the Mayans, the eagle that flies high in the sky toward the Sun symbolized heavenly power. The Aborigines of Australia believed the eagle carried the souls of the dead back to the spirit world. In medieval Europe in the Christian religion, the eagle came to represent prayer ascending to God.

Snakes

Snakes are seen as destructive and evil, sly and cunning, but also as creatures with power over life and death. In Christianity, the snake represents the devil. Ancient Egyptians worshiped several snake-headed gods and goddesses, all with different roles and jobs. The Pueblo Indians of South America saw snakes as symbols of lightning and used zigzag-shaped "snake sticks" in rain-making ceremonies.

In classical mythology, the eagle was associated with Zeus, god of lightning. It was therefore thought that the eagle could never be struck by lightning.

Cats

In times past, the cat was linked with many gods or worshiped as one itself. In Siam it was believed that the soul of a king passed into a cat when he died. The soul then rested during the cat's life, and went on to paradise after the cat's death. Bastet was an ancient Egyptian goddess with a cat's head.

Bees

Bees have been part of many religions, mostly as symbols of immortality and rebirth. In ancient Egypt, bees were seen as the "tears of Ra," the Sun god. The "Great Mother" of ancient Greece was known as the queen bee and her priestesses were called "melissae," the bees. The bee is also an emblem of Cupid and Kama, both gods of love.

As a bird of prey the eagle is one of the most powerful birds in the sky.

The dog-headed god often stood guard outside ancient Egyptian tombs.

Ram

In ancient Egypt, the Sun god Ra was addressed as "thou ram, mightiest of created things." Each year, during the Feast of Optet, a boat was decorated with rams' heads. A ram was also sacrificed to the god Amon at Thebes.

Anubis

The Egyptian god of the dead, Anubis had the body of a priest and the head of a jackal. He guided the souls of the dead to the "hall of judgement" where their hearts were weighed against the "feather of truth."

Water

THE ELEMENT WATER has always symbolized the emotions and the deep, subconscious world of our dreams, inner hopes, and fears. Just as the world of our inner self and instincts is often mysterious to us, so the world of the deep oceans and the creatures that live there is one we know little about, and find it hard to enter. Here, in the ocean depths, there are creatures as alien to us as those from another planet. Water covers more than two-thirds of our planet and is home to millions of creatures, some of whom have senses and abilities we will never have.

MILLIONS OF YEARS AGO, LIFE BEGAN AS MINUTE BACTERIA IN THE WORLD'S WATERY ENVIRONMENT.

OVER 500 VARIETIES OF FISH HAVE SPECIAL, STACKS OF CELLS THAT CAN PRODUCE ELECTRICITY.

THE ANTARCTIC PROVIDES THE OCEANS WITH OXYGEN-RICH WATER TO SUPPORT A VAST ARRAY OF LIFE.

The Great Change

Salmon were often seen as fish from the "Otherworld," able to change from one form to another. One Irish folk tale tells of a soldier who laughed that the salmon was held in such awe. He vowed to catch one and eat it for his supper. He did catch one, but when he took out his knife, it turned into a beautiful woman. Also in the Celtic legend of Tuan MacCarell, the magical qualities of the salmon are kept alive. Tuan comes to Ireland as a salmon, is captured and eaten, and reborn as a man.

Salmon

IN MANY CULTURES salmon are considered to be magical and inspirational fish. This idea has probably grown out of the tremendous changes salmon go through during their lives. After a heroic journey home from the sea to breed and lay its eggs, the salmon's body changes rapidly and ages at a fantastic rate. In a few days, having given all its life-energy to its children, the Pacific salmon dies, showing that new life is born from death—one of the great mysteries of life.

Again and again the salmon jumps up rapids and waterfalls, using its strong and flexible body to reach home.

MOST OF THE WORLD belongs to the salmon, for two thirds of the world is covered by water and the salmon is at home in both salt water and freshwater. A salmon lays its eggs in the gravel bed of an inland stream. When the fry hatch, they are only a fraction of an inch (a centimeter) long and feed off the food stored in their mother's yolk sac. Some months later, the still tiny salmon are seized by an ancient urge and start to move

WHEN CARRIED BY THE CURRENT TO THE SEA, SALMON GO TAIL FIRST.

downstream: from the sparkling stream to the broad, deep river until finally they reach the sea. Out in the vastness of the Pacific or Atlantic Oceans, it is only the strongest of the salmon that survive. Between one and five years later, the fish that was once the size of a sardine, now 18 in (45 cm) of gleaming silver, begins the great journey home.

Somehow, someway, the salmon finds its way from the oceans, to the exact spot in the quiet stream where it was born. All the way back is uphill, against the current, so the salmon must use all its strength to push on and not be swept back to sea. It keeps going, not stopping to eat, and avoiding

SPECIAL FISH LADDERS HELP SALMON OVERCOME BARRIERS ON THEIR JOURNEYS UPSTREAM.

fishing vessels sweeping the mouths of rivers with their nets, and fishermen and animals such as grizzly bears, otters, and mink on the lookout for a fish supper. As if that isn't hard enough, the salmon has to jump, like an acrobat, up rapids and waterfalls. It can jump a waterfall 10 ft (3 m) high in one leap, but at a larger fall looks for rocky ledges and leaps up in stages. The salmon may fall back many times, but it won't give up—something stronger than weariness and

the need to rest drives it on and it moves magnificently to meet its fate.

As a spiritual warrior battles to overcome obstacles and dangers on its "quest," the salmon struggles and endures, using

IN ANCIENT BRITAIN, THE SALMON WAS GUARDIAN OF WELLS, POOLS, AND STREAMS.

strength, wit, and determination to swim back, sometimes thousands of miles (kilometers,) to where it began. At last the salmon reaches its home ground where it chooses a mate who has made the same journey. Here, where its own life began, its children are born to start their own adventurous journey through life.

Salmon Power

A Dakotan Indian chief had a beautiful daughter. He sent out a challenge that whoever was strong enough to break the pair of elk's antlers that hung in his lodge, could marry his daughter. All the animals and birds tried, but their strength and skill were not enough. The only creature left was the salmon, he broke the antlers into five pieces and, claiming his prize, led the beautiful daughter away!

Little Helpers

Sighted salmon have been seen guiding blind salmon by swimming close to them and pushing them in the right direction. One pair were seen to have a code: a push near the tail meant turn right, and one near the head, turn left.

SALMON ADVENTURE

A salmon, taken from a hatchery in Humboldt County, California, U.S. was released into a coastal stream 5½ miles (9 km) away, to see if it could return to the tank in which it was born. After swimming up a small stream and under a large highway, the salmon reached a sewer. Here it went up 80 ft (24 m) to a small water channel. At the end of the channel was a 4 in (10 cm) drain pipe, which rose vertically 2½ ft (76 cm). The salmon jumped up the drain pipe and into the outlet pipe that led to its tank. However, here it found that the outlet pipe had a cap on. After a few attempts, the salmon knocked off the cap and finally arrived back at the tank in which it was born!

Octopuses

ONE OF THE MOST feared sea-creatures in the oceans, octopuses were often called the devil-fish. Many untruths about their fierceness are believed, but in fact they are very shy animals and usually keep away from any animal larger than themselves. If frightened, an octopus may change from one color to another, much as we might blush or turn pale.

Blue-ringed Octopus

The blue-ringed octopus is just 4 in (10 cm) across, but in Australia, it kills more people each year than sharks do. However, it is shy like other octopuses, and only attacks if it is picked up or disturbed. When it bites with its parrot-like beak, it kills its prey with a poisonous saliva. The salivary glands produce enzymes called proteases, which partially digest food before it reaches the stomach.

Giant Squid

In the 1930s, the Brunswick, a 15,000 ton (15,287 tonne) tanker owned by the Royal Norwegian Navy, was attacked three times by a giant squid. Each time the squid wrapped its tentacles around the hull and tried to pull the ship down.

During World War II, a British Admiralty trawler was anchored in the Indian Ocean, near the Maldive Islands. One of the crew who was standing on the deck fishing, saw a green, glowing light in the water. He realized he was looking into the eye of a huge squid. The sailor claimed that the squid lay alongside the 175 ft (53 m) ship, over-reaching it at either end.

Octopuses have more efficient eyes than humans because they don't have a blind spot. They also have twice as many light-sensitive cells, so can probably see much more detail.

OCTOPUSES LIKE TO find hidey-holes and manage to ooze their great bodies through the smallest gaps into empty clam shells, discarded bottles, and cracks in rocks. They may stay in these tight spaces for weeks, returning to them after hunting trips, not always coming back from the same direction, and making detours to avoid new obstacles.

AN OCTOPUS HAS A RING OF EIGHT ARMS AROUND ITS MOUTH.

Their ability to make judgements in new situations, makes octopuses the most intelligent of invertebrates. They learn from their success and failures and apply what they learn to solve problems. This particularly applies to situations where a good spatial memory and navigational skills are needed.

Seahorses

ONE OF nature's anomalies, seahorses are fish without scales—their bodies are covered with an armor of tough, bony plates. A seahorse swims with the body held vertically, and propels itself along by a tiny, yellow-tinged fin on its back, fluttering it so fast it is almost invisible.

Seahorses wrap their tails around plants and change color to match the scenery.

THESE LITTLE creatures have the arched neck and head of a horse, the grasping tail of a monkey, and the chameleon's ability to change color. Their eyes move independently, so they are able to look in two directions at once.

There are more than 40 species of seahorse, ranging from 1 in (2.5 cm) to 2 ft

WHEN SEAHORSES ARE BORN, THEY ARE SO TRANSPARENT THEIR HEARTS CAN BE SEEN BEATING.

(60 cm) in length. They live in almost every warm sea in the world, and are found in a whole range of colors. One of the slowest moving life forms

in the sea, most seahorses never move above 0.01 mph (0.016 kph.)

An unusual seahorse characteristic is that the male, not the female, incubates the baby seahorses. The male has a pouch like a kangaroo, in which the female lays her eggs. For 45 days he watches over his children-to-be, until, one day, a tiny, perfect little seahorse pops out of the pouch, closely followed by another and another, until hundreds drift toward the surface of the water, rather like confetti.

Bubble Buoyancy

Even in its calm, slow-moving life, the seahorse has one thing to avoid—getting a puncture! The seahorse keeps afloat with an internal balloon full of gas. If just one tiny bubble of gas escapes this buoyancy bladder, the seahorse sinks helplessly to the seabed. There the seahorse must sit until it has made enough gas to fill up its tank and refloat itself.

Black Magic

In ancient times, the Greeks thought the seahorse was capable of black magic. Wine with a seahorse soaking in it was a powerful poison, and the ashes of a seahorse, if mixed with honey and vinegar, were used as an antidote to other poisons. The Roman writer, Pliny, advised using seahorse ashes to cure baldness, skin rashes, and the bite of a mad dog!

STRUGGLE FOR SURVIVAL

Despite its wonderful ability to camouflage itself by blending in with the surroundings, the seahorse still has a struggle to survive. Each pair of seahorses produces thousands of young, but on average only two of those babies survive to adulthood. Then, if they do avoid being caught by tuna fish, crabs, skates, and rays, the seahorses have to hang on for grim death. Each time a storm blows up, their fragile bodies may be torn from whatever they are clinging to, battered in the waves, cast ashore, or they may simply die from exhaustion. Should they escape all these dangers, the seahorses may well be caught to become pets in a fish tank.

Turtles and terrapins

MOST TURTLES AND TERRAPINS, like their land-living relatives, tortoises, move slowly on land. Their bodies are not well supported by their legs, so much of their weight rests on the ground. Turtles and terrapins are "at home" anywhere because they carry their homes on their backs. When threatened, most kinds of turtles can withdraw into their shells and are protected.

Turtle Rescue

In March 1991, a sailor from South Korea fell overboard a cargo ship. While in the water, the sailor kept afloat by holding onto a turtle's shell for six hours. When the sailor was rescued by another boat, the turtle was also hauled aboard. Here it was given a meal of meat and bananas before being returned to the sea.

Racing Turtle

Long ago a rabbit and a turtle had a race. They crossed valleys and high hills, the rabbit running as hard as it could, but each time it passed the turtle it soon found the turtle ahead again. In the end, the rabbit was exhausted and the turtle plodded on and won. How? There was only one rabbit, but a different turtle at the top of each hill!

On land most marine turtles move by alternating movements of their limbs, as most four-legged animals do.

TURTLES AND TERRAPINS live all over the world in both freshwater and salt water, or on land near marshes, swamps, and in forests. Like tortoises, they are reptiles that have an ancestry older than the dinosaurs.

Their skeleton evolved as a protective horny shell, the upper part of which is supported by the ribs and backbone. The largest turtle in the world is the leatherback turtle, which can grow to a weight of 800 lb (360 kg.) Its flippers have a

THE STINKPOT TURTLE GIVES OFF A BAD SMELL WHEN THREATENED.

maximum span of 9 ft (2.5 m.)

Most female turtles lay their eggs and bury them in pits of sand or earth. When the eggs hatch, the young turtles dig their way out to the surface. The female green turtle, a type of marine turtle, travels hundreds of miles (kilometers) to the beach of its own birth to lay its eggs. Using its foreflippers, it sweeps

Creation Story

Many tribal creation stories say that the Earth was born on the back of a turtle. The Native Americans refer to North America as Turtle Island because their legends say that when the world was covered with water, the turtle plunged to the bottom of the oceans and brought the Earth up on its back so that people could have a safe, dry home.

away sand to create a hollow for its body. The turtle then lies over the hollow, its shell flush with the beach and digs a hole about 16 in (40.5 cm) deep beneath its tail. It lays the eggs in the hole and after covering them with sand, returns to the sea.

Two to three months later, the young turtles hatch, surface, and

Pond turtles hibernate in winter, burying themselves in specially built chambers in the river bank.

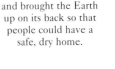

ADELITA'S JOURNEY

Adelita, a loggerhead turtle, was tagged with an electronic signalling device by researchers at the University of Arizona, U.S., then released into the sea on August 10th, 1996, just off the coast of Santa Rosalita, a small town in Mexico. Adelita was the only one of the many tagged turtles, and the purpose of the research was to show that turtles make very long journeys to the beaches where they want to lay their eggs. At New Year, Adelita was just north of Hawaii and by July 31st, 1997 had arrived in Japan, a journey of 9,000 miles (15, 000 km)—a very long swim for a turtle!

SOME RIVER TURTLES CAN STAY UNDERWATER FOR MANY HOURS WITHOUT COMING UP FOR AIR.

SNAPPING TURTLES ARE HIGHLY AGGRESSIVE, SHOOTING THEIR HEADS FORWARD WITH SPEED.

rush to the sea. Unfortunately not many survive. The houses and hotels on the beach fronts are usually brightly lit at night. This confuses the young turtles, which find their way back to the sea by light reflecting from the water, and they wander toward the shore lights instead.

Today many turtles are rare and have become protected species. They are hunted for their meat, hides, and eggs or captured and sold as pets.

The Turtle House

A "turtle house" is a place at the bottom of the ocean where turtles go to be cleaned by a variety of fish. The turtles turn up regularly and sit contentedly, flippers tucked under, eyes shut, while fish, such as the surgeonfish, pick away at their shells to clean them. A turtle that is enjoying its grooming may stick its head straight up to let the fish know it wants its neck cleaned.

Shark Teeth

Sharks use their teeth to bite and tear and grind their food, but they don't chew. Most sharks have more than four rows of teeth. The front row do all the work, and as they wear down a spare row rolls outward to replace them. Sharks get a new set of teeth approximately every two weeks. One shark may have up to 24,000 teeth in its lifetime

Man Shark

Some ancient kings were shown in pictures as half human, half shark. The British Museum in London, U.K. has bronze reliefs of the King of Benin shown in this way, and the Trocadero, in Paris, France displays statues of the Kings of Dahomey as sharks with scaled bodies. Also, the Fijian President, Ratu Sir Ganilau, was said to be descended from the shark god Dakuwaqa. After his death in December 1993, a boat carrying his coffin left Suva Harbour in Fiji accompanied by a school of sharks.

Remora

Despite their fierce reputation, sharks do have some friends—ones who literally hang on and go everywhere with them. Remora are tiny fish that attach themselves to sharks by means of suction pads on their heads. They earn their keep by cleaning parasites from a shark's skin. One shark may have two or more remoras on it, showing its status as a hunter who can provide free food for others.

Sharks

THE SHARK HAS been swimming in the oceans of the world for 350 million years and its image as a vicious predator is written deep in the human consciousness. Its sense of smell is incredibly keen—the shark can pick up and follow a scent as dilute as one part to 50 million parts of water. The shark is also sensitive to vibrations in the water and is particularly attracted by erratic movements.

SHARKS HAVE a reputation for killing humans, yet fewer than 100 shark attacks a year are reported worldwide and most attacks don't cause serious injuries. The bull shark is one of the only sharks to come into shallow water, and is responsible for many of the attacks on humans. Other dangerous sharks are the hammerhead, the tiger, the mako, the blue shark, and the

A GREAT WHITE SHARK CAN GROW TO UP TO 20 FT (6 M) LONG.

carpet shark. The carpet shark lies on the sea bed looking so much like part of the ocean floor that swimmers may step on it by mistake and provoke an attack. The great white shark is the most feared and fiercest killer in our oceans. It is often called the "white death." Not many people ever see it as it rarely comes into shallow water where people swim.

Sharks have no enemies except other sharks and humans, although dolphins can kill sharks in some instances.

It is true that sharks are efficient killing machines that have been evolving and adapting for 400 million years. A shark can hear from 1 mile (1.5 km) away, smell and feel vibrations from 300 ft (91 m), and see from 89 ft (27 m.) In fact, a shark can follow the

A BASKING SHARK SWIMS WITH ITS MOUTH OPEN WIDE LETTING PLANKTON DRIFT INSIDE.

smell of blood across miles (kilometers) of ocean.

There are over 250 species of sharks and the numbers of many species are falling rapidly because of hunting and fishing by humans. One hundred and sixty-four thousand, three hundred sharks are killed every day—that's 6,845 each hour, or two every second. Their meat is used for food, their livers for oil, the cartilage in health

Moses Sole

When Moses parted the waters of the Red Sea to let the Israelites cross, legend says a small fish was caught in the middle and flattened. Called the Moses sole, these fish give off a milky liquid that is an ideal shark repellent. The liquid from the fish is poisonous to sharks and paralyzes them.

WHAT AN APPETITE

While dissecting a gray shark, vets found the hindquarters of a pig, eight legs of mutton, the front half of a dog, and 300 lb (136 kg) of horsemeat in its stomach. Other reports tell how the crew of an old steamer, fed one shark with newspapers, a biscuit tin, a brick wrapped in a piece of cloth, a sack of coal, a wooden crate, and a broken alarm clock! Other items, for example, shoes, wallets, bits of other sharks, a driver's license, dogs, a cow's hoof, the antlers of a deer, a chicken coop with feathers and bones still inside it, and a chest of drawers have all been recovered from sharks' stomachs!

SOME SHARKS CAN DETECT BLOOD FROM OVER 1/4 MILE (0.5 KM) AWAY.

A hammerhead's eyes are positioned on the outer edges of its hammer-shaped head. This may help it see more at the side and behind its head.

foods, and other body parts in drugs and cosmetics. Six million blue sharks are caught annually by mistake, mixed up in the catches of deep sea fishing vessels. Sharks maintain the balance between the different fish species. When they are taken out of the sea food chain, many fish become scarce, because they are eaten by other fish that were formerly eaten by sharks.

The great white shark has razor-sharp, triangular serrated teeth.

Whales

W HEN THE VOYAGER spacecraft traveled
out to the stars carrying the message that
life exists on Earth, many sounds of life on
Earth were included: music, the sound of a
person's thoughts, greetings in 60 different
languages, and the song of the humpbacked
whale. Whale sounds span a broad range of
frequencies, the lowest of which is well below
the level that a human ear can pick up.

Whale Breath

Whales breathe air, so when
they are below water, they
must hold their breath.
Some whales can hold their
breath for up to 45 minutes.
When they come up to
take in more air, the air they
breathe out is hot and as
it hits the colder air outside
it condenses into a column
of vapor as much as
15 ft (4.5 m) high. This is
what you see when a
whale "spouts."

Sucking Fish

Sucking Fish, also known
as the remora fish, challenged
the whale to a race. The whale
thought this hilarious and
agreed. Grampus, the fastest
swimmer in the sea, was to
swim ahead and act as the
judge, but just as the race
started, Sucking Fish hid under
Grampus's fin. When the whale
arrived, Sucking Fish was
already there. As a prize
the whale agreed to carry
him, and to this day
the remora fish travel
attached to the whale.

*The humpback whale has
a curved lower jaw and
approximately 22
throat grooves.*

WHALES TALK TO EACH other
by whistles and chirps. A blue
whale's whistle can be 188
decibels—that's louder than the
noise made by an air plane. The
male humpback whale can sing
non-stop for half an hour or more.
Often members of a group sing
the same song, repeating it note
for note, beat for beat, exactly.
Sometimes a group of whales
leaves the winter waters and
swims south in the middle of a
song. When the group returns,
six months later, it will pick up
the song again, as if there had
been no interruption. The songs
change and are added to month
by month, year by year, as if the
whales sing their own history
as they make it.

The U.S. biologist, Roger
Payne, calculated that using
the deep ocean sound
channel, two whales making

**THE BLUE WHALE IS THE
LARGEST MAMMAL EVER TO HAVE
LIVED ON EARTH.**

very low frequency sounds could communicate with each other on opposite sides of the world.

For most of their history the whales, who don't have language as we do, and don't have hands to signal, have communicated with

each other through the vastness of the deep oceans by singing their songs. However, we cut them off from each other with our noise pollution: our boat engines, mechanical sonars, weapons tests, and low-flying aircraft. Wherever they go in deep water there is unnatural, artificial noise, 24 hours a day, every day. Research has shown that gray whales off the coast of California, U.S. divert miles (kilometers) to avoid loud sound sources. There is nowhere they can go to get away from

THE MALE NARWHAL HAS A LONG SPIRAL TUSK GROWING FROM ITS MOUTH.

it, except shallow water, which may be why so many whales are found stranded on the beaches.

By sending out sounds and receiving back echoes from the objects around, whales use echolocation to find their food, their way, and each other. Sound and the force of a vibration is magnified underwater. For creatures with sensitive hearing that live in such a noise polluted environment, it is torture.

In 1992, it was thought that whales found off Newfoundland, Canada, may have had damaged ear structures after underwater blasting was used in constructing oil rigs. Without their ears whales are "blind." The oceans of the world belong to the creatures of the oceans. If we wish to share them, we should do so with care and compassion.

SPERM WHALES MAKE DEEP DIVES OF UP TO 3,300 FT (1,000 M) TO FIND FOOD.

STAR OF THE EAST

The *Star of the East*, a whaling ship, was sailing out near the Falkland Islands in 1891, when its crew spotted a whale. Two small boats were launched to harpoon the whale. In the struggle that followed, two sailors went overboard. One was drowned and the body of the other disappeared. Eventually the whale was killed and cut open. Inside, they found one of the missing crewman, James Bartley, unconscious, but still alive. Amazingly, Bartley recovered from his ordeal, although it took some weeks, but his skin had been bleached white by the acids in the whale's stomach. It stayed that way for the rest of his life!

Whale Island

In many cultures, the whale is said to support the Earth on its back and so when it moves, there are earthquakes. In Slav folklore, four whales support the Earth. There are also many popular legends of sailors mistaking a whale's back for an island, landing on it, and lighting a fire to cook food. The whale, feeling the heat, plunged into the ocean and the sailors drowned.

Whale Birth

Whales are born tail first. Like most mammals, they breathe air, and if their babies were born head first they would drown. As soon as a baby whale is born, its mother and sometimes another whale, helps it to the surface to take its first breath of air.

Dolphin Symbols

As long ago as 2200 B.C. dolphins appeared in cave paintings in Norway. The walls of the Aegean Palace of Knossos, in Greece, are covered with dolphin frescoes. All across the world, from the East to Asia and Western Europe, dolphin images have been found on coins, pottery, statues, and tales of them recorded in stories and songs. Roman coins dated 74 B.C. show a boy riding a dolphin.

Good Teachers

At the Society for Environmental Awareness, in Key Largo, Florida, U.S. dolphins voluntarily work with children with severe learning difficulties, playing gently with them in sea-water pools. After a session with dolphins, the children show greater interest in their surroundings and often have a creativity spurt. They also show improved communication, increased learning skills, and positive behavior changes after spending time with dolphins.

Dolphins

THE DOLPHIN IS NATURE'S ambassador. So many times throughout history dolphins have reversed the law of the wild and sought out humans, rather than fled from them. There are many recorded tales of dolphins saving humans from drowning, befriending them, and then carrying them on their backs. Pliny, the Roman historian, tells of a wild dolphin that took a boy for a ride at Hippo, a Roman settlement in Africa.

WHY DO WILD DOLPHINS come into the bays and inlets of our shores to seek contact with humans? Why do so many people who meet dolphins talk of feeling love and friendship coming from the dolphins to them? Many people who work with dolphins believe that they give off an energy, the Japanese call it "chi energy," which rebalances and heals us. In ancient Greece, to kill a dolphin was a crime punishable by death.

There are 32 species of this mammal that belongs to the whale family. They are found in all the world's oceans and some rivers in tropical countries. Long and streamlined, their colorings and markings vary, but most have the familiar long beak and bulging forehead. Inside the bulge is a pad of fat called the "melon," which is thought to help focus their sonar beams. The bottlenose

DOLPHINS ARE REALLY SMALL-TOOTHED WHALES.

THE BOTTLENOSE DOLPHIN IS HIGHLY INTELLIGENT. IT IS OFTEN USED TO PERFORM IN ZOOS.

dolphin has a curved mouth leading into a lower jaw that projects beyond the upper jaw, giving its well-known "smile." The dolphin's skin is sensitive to touch and is easily scarred.

Like whales, dolphins navigate and communicate using sounds. By forcing air past valves and flaps located just below its blowhole, a dolphin can make at least 32 different sounds, including whistles, clicks, squawks, barks, and groans. However, its high frequency clicks do not carry as far underwater as the low frequency noises made by whales.

Many of the sounds are too high for humans to hear, so we need instruments that detect and register them. The whistling language by which they talk has been named "delphinese" by scientists.

DOLPHINS ARE BORN TAIL-, NOT HEAD-FIRST, UNLIKE MOST OTHER MAMMALS.

Navigation System

A dolphin navigates by making clicking sounds, which bounce off objects ahead and are echoed back. Many dolphins get trapped and die in fishing nets because the holes in the nets don't offer a surface for the echo to bounce off, and the dolphins think there is no obstacle ahead.

OPERATION SUNFLOWER

In 1974, Dr. Horace Dobbs swam in the sea with a wild dolphin. That encounter changed his life, and the lives of many others, for Dr. Dobbs founded the International Dolphin Watch, an organization that studies wild dolphins. In the late 1980s, Dr. Dobbs took Bill, a man ill with depression since 1974, to meet Simo, a wild dolphin off the Welsh coast. After swimming with Simo, Bill said he felt much love. The next day, after years of not wanting to go outside, Bill rushed out of the hotel down to the harbor to meet the dolphin. In the wake of this, "Operation Sunflower" was set up, in which severely depressed people are taken to spend time with wild dolphins.

Dolphins swim fast and feed by making shallow dives. They surface several times a minute.

Crabs

THE ANCIENT GREEK word for crab was "karkinos" and its Latin name is "cancer." Both of these names come from the early Indian word "crenate," meaning to break or crush. For some reason crabs have always had a bad reputation. The crab's huge pincer claws have probably caused this, but in spite of its appearance, the crab is not vicious and will try and avoid humans if possible.

CRABS VARY IN SIZE greatly, from just $1/2$ in (1.25 cm) to the giant crab of Japan, which may span 16 in (40 cm) from claw tip to claw tip.

Sea creatures do not need supporting skeletons like land dwellers, because the water itself supports them. Large spider crabs do not come on land because, unsupported by water, they cannot move their long legs. However, water is more difficult

backward. Most of its joints are like our knee joints and can only bend in one direction.

The type of claws a crab has is a clue to its way of life. Slow-moving crabs that feed on mollusks have strong claws to crack shells. In fact, the claws of a morro crab are so powerful that they can crush a man's hand. Those that rely on catching moving prey have claws with serrated edges.

THE FIDDLER CRAB HAS A HUGE MENACING-LOOKING LEFT CLAW.

to move through than air, so the shapes of sea creatures have evolved to create the least resistance when moving. This is why the crab's body is streamlined and flattened.

Most crabs don't swim, but walk or run across the ocean bed. A crab can scuttle sideways much faster than it can move forward or

Hermit Crabs

Hermit crabs live in empty mollusk shells. Often they take in a lodger—a sea anemone. The anemone attaches itself to the top of the shell and acts as a bodyguard, using its stinging tentacles to scare off predators. When the crab moves to a larger shell, it taps the anemone as a warning, and moves it to the new home.

Heike

In A.D. 12, two Japanese noble families, the Heike and the Genji, fought for years to rule Japan. The tyrannical Heike were finally defeated in the naval battle of Dannoura in the straits of Shimonoseki, and in disgrace threw themselves into the sea where they were transformed into crabs. Since then crabs are supposed to have Heike features on their shells.

Crustacean Symbols

To Buddhists, the crab symbolizes the sleep of death. In Africa it is a symbol of evil. In the East, a lobster is a good omen, and is often shown without claws. In ancient Greece it was considered sacred, and in China was a sign of wealth and a happy marriage.

Route March

In Jamaica, land crabs live in rock crevices. Once a year they head for the beaches to breed. Long lines of crabs march purposefully toward the sea, scrambling over anything in their path, even houses.

Lobsters

LOBSTERS, LIKE CRABS, HAVE skeletons on the outside of their bodies, enclosing their internal organs in a natural armor, to which the muscles are attached on the inside. Lobsters come in many colors: yellow, gray, greenish-brown, dusty orange, blue, and spotted.

THE LOBSTER was made inside out and upside down. Not only does it carry its skeleton on the outside of the body, most of the nervous system is along its belly instead of its back, and its kidneys are behind its forehead. A lobster's brain, which is around the size of a pinhead, is in two parts, one above and one below its throat. It listens with its legs, through tiny sensory hairs that pick up underwater vibrations, and tastes with its antennae and leg-like mouthparts.

Lobsters grow by shedding (molting) and replacing their shells 25 to 30 times in the first seven years of life. When molting, the lobster hides in a rocky crevice and waits, eating nothing. Gradually its body and muscles become flabby and

A LOBSTER'S TEETH ARE IN ITS STOMACH.

powerless. The shell splits, and the defenseless lobster struggles out. Now extremely soft and vulnerable, its body absorbs water until after a few hours it is much larger. The new shell hardens rapidly and after three days the lobster is ready to leave its hideaway.

Lost Legs

Would you notice if an arm or leg fell off? Probably! A lobster can lose a walking leg, a claw, or an antenna, and carry on as if nothing has happened. In fact, it can discard one deliberately to escape a predator and later grow it back. Biologists say this indicates a primitive nervous system, and less sensitivity to pain than humans or other species.

Lobsters' Trail

Lobsters tend to stay in one place, but each fall lobsters in the Bahamas move from reefs to deeper water. To cross open areas, they form a long column of 50 or more. Each lobster hooks its front legs around the tail of the lobster in front, and then they go across the seabed faster than a person can swim. One tagged column traveled a record distance of 225 miles (362 km.)

Lobsters and crabs are scavengers. They eat all kinds of rubbish and left-overs from the seabed. They also eat fish and shellfish.

Crocodiles

Toothy Grin

A crocodile may have around 40 teeth set in the sockets of its large jawbones. When closed the jaws interlock, giving the crocodile a powerful grip on its prey. As soon as the sharp points of a crocodile's teeth wear down, the teeth are replaced by new ones growing behind. When the Nile crocodile has finished a meal, it takes a nap with its mouth open. This is the cue for a little bird called the spur-winged plover to hop inside and clean the crocodile's dirty teeth.

CROCODILE FOSSILS have been found dating back to before 65 million years ago—the same time that dinosaurs walked the Earth. In fact, crocodiles are direct descendants of the prehistoric archosaurs. Crocodiles are clever reptiles, they learn fast and can move with lightning speed.

DESPITE BEING SMART for a reptile, a crocodile has a very small brain. The crocodile uses stealth and strength to catch and overpower its prey. Lying still in the water, it often looks as harmless as a floating log. Then, when a deer or small mammal comes to the riverbank to drink, with a mighty sweep of its tail, the crocodile knocks the creature

long jaws shut with a force strong enough to crush the bones of a small animal. However, once closed, the jaw muscles are so weak in opening that a human can hold its mouth shut with one hand. Intimidating as its teeth are, they are geared for clamping, not

CROCODILES' EYES SHINE RED IN THE DARK.

down, seizes it and holds it underwater until it drowns. One third of a crocodile's weight is in its tail.

A crocodile will attack anything that goes near the water. It is an opportunist, seizing any meal that passes its way—so dangling arms and legs are in danger of being grabbed. A crocodile can crash its

A crocodile drags its prey underwater and twists round and round to tear off chunks of flesh.

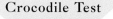

Crocodile Test

In days of old, one Arabian test of innocence was called the "Ordeal by Crocodile." During an "Ordeal by Crocodile," accused people were thrown into a pit of crocodiles. If the accused came out unharmed, they were innocent, if not, they were guilty. Needless to say most folk were found guilty! In west Africa, just to be attacked by a crocodile was a sign of guilt. This was because crocodiles were thought to be the souls of murdered people seeking their revenge.

chewing. Nile crocodiles work together to catch food, forming a dam with their bodies to trap fish. With larger prey, one crocodile holds it down while the other rips it apart.

A crocodile is nature's submarine. The crocodile has a system of valves that automatically close when it dives to protect its ears, nose, and throat from water. The eyes sit on top of the head and stay above water when the rest of the body is submerged. A crocodile can stay underwater for as long as an hour.

When swimming underwater, thousands of tiny crystals embedded in a crocodile's eyes collect light and allow it amazing underwater vision. A crocodile does not use its feet as paddles to swim, but swings its tail from side to side to push back the water and propel itself along at high speed.

The average crocodile can have around 10–15 lb (4.5–7 kg) of stones in its stomach at any one time. A crocodile swallows stones to give itself the added weight needed to stay underwater, and also to help grind up its food.

American alligators live in swamps. In the dry season, when the swamps dry up, they live in holes in the ground which stay damp.

Crocs and Alligators

A crocodile has a larger snout than an alligator and when its jaws are shut, the fourth tooth on each side of its lower jaw sticks out. An alligator has no teeth showing. The word "alligator" comes from the Spanish for lizard "el largato." Try saying this fast a few times and it sounds just like "alligator." An alligator is smaller than a crocodile, and is found only in the Americas.

CROCODILE TEARS

It was thought long ago, that a crocodile moaned and sighed, like a person in distress in order to lure its prey. Whatever or whoever came to investigate the pitiful sound was snatched and devoured. One Indian belief is that a crocodile begins to eat the body of its victim, hangs over its prey, then "sheds tears" before finishing the meal. This is probably where the term "crocodile tears" comes from. In truth, a crocodile only eats what it can swallow whole, so often drags its prey to an underwater lair and leaves the body to rot until it is soft enough to swallow.

Frogs and toads

Water-holding Frog

On the rare occasion when rain comes to the deserts of central Australia, the water-holding frog shoots out from its underground home and, using loose skin to form bags, collects more than half its own weight in water. As the next rainfall in the desert may not be for five or six years, the frog stores this water by oozing a membrane-like envelope around itself to seal in the water.

Frog Parliament

The croaking of a group of frogs is often called a "frog parliament," meaning a lot of noise, without much being achieved! Long ago the frog parliament asked the Greek god Zeus to give it a king. A king was provided and the first thing he did was to throw a log into the frogs' pool. The log landed with a splash and impressed the frogs, but after a while the king became lazy. The frogs grew tired of a king who did nothing, and asked for another. This time Zeus sent a stork, who gobbled them all up!

Frogs use their powerful back legs to leap from lily pad to lily pad looking for flies to eat.

FROGS AND TOADS belong to a group of animals called amphibians. This means they are able to live both in water and on land. Hundreds of years ago, these small creatures were thought to be lucky, and to kill one was believed to bring bad luck. Perhaps this is because neither the frog nor the toad are likely to be far from fresh water, and as water is so precious, the sight of a frog or toad was a good sign.

IN ANCIENT EGYPT FROGS were used as symbols of new life and resurrection. This may be because a frog changes form very dramatically during the early stages of its life. From one of a jelly-like mass of eggs, it grows into a tadpole—a round, black body with gills on either side of its neck, a tail, and no legs. Gradually the tail shrinks away to nothing, and legs start to grow.

Amazing though this is, a greater change now takes place—the oxygen-absorbing gills gradually disappear and lungs grow inside the body instead.

Living both on land and in water and having a delicate, porous skin through which it takes in oxygen, the frog is easily affected by fertilizers, pesticides, and chemical pollutants in water and rain, and by changes in the ozone layer, which allow more ultraviolet radiation through to

THERE ARE OVER 2,500 SPECIES OF FROG AND TOAD.

the planet. This can cause mutations (genetic changes) resulting in some frogs being born with missing eyes, missing or deformed limbs, and, in some cases, extra pairs of legs.

Frogs and toads are gardeners' friends as they eat many of the creatures that damage garden plants. Their diets are slightly

A FROG'S SKIN IS ALWAYS MOIST, EVEN IN DRY WEATHER.

different, so they can survive happily on the same patch of ground. Both eat beetles, flies, and woodlice, but a toad will gobble up ants, while a frog prefers slugs and snails. When a tasty insect comes into sight, the frog flips the back of its tongue over and forward, shooting it out of its mouth with speed to grab its meal.

A frog's skin is not actually slimy, but it is always moist, even in dry weather, because it contains special glands which produce secretions to keep it moist, smooth, and supple. Toads have a tougher, drier, warty skin.

SOME FROGS AND TOADS ARE POISONOUS.

This means they are unable to "breathe" through their skins as frogs do, but they survive better on land in dry places.

The common toad hides during the daytime, emerging only at dusk to feed on flies and other insects.

Strange Weather

Throughout history, there have been strange reports of it "raining" frogs and toads. On September 24, 1973, *The Times* newspaper, from the U.K., reported that the day before tens of thousands of small toads rained from the sky onto the French village of Brignoles. In a letter dated October 24, 1683, John Collinges, a Quaker scholar, tells of toads raining on Acle, U.K. and running into the houses in the village. In A.D. 4, the Roman writer Pliny wrote of a shower of frogs that blocked Greek roads for days.

PRESERVED ALIVE

Frogs and toads seem to have an almost miraculous ability to survive for huge lengths of time holed up in tiny spaces. In 1719, the French Academy of Sciences reported that a toad "middle-sized, but lean and filling up the whole vacant space" was found in a cavity inside the trunk of an elm. In 1851, a frog, found alive inside a piece of coal, was shown at the Great Exhibition, London, U.K., and in 1865, the Leeds Mercury, a newspaper from the U.K. reported that a live toad had been found in a 200 million year old block of limestone quarried at Hartlepool Waterworks, U.K. It is not known how the animal found its way into the block.

Icy Duck

Ducks have been seen helping each other when injured and in trouble. Once a duck was spotted with its feet frozen into the ice of a frozen pond. It was quacking in distress, but before any onlookers could help, a group of ducks rushed up and began fussing around the trapped duck's feet. Eventually, the extra heat caused by the ducks walking on the ice melted it, and the duck was set free.

Father Goose

The parents of some ducklings living on a city lake were killed, but luckily the ducklings were adopted by a gander (male goose.) Each day, the gander led the ducklings to a nearby house, where bread was put out for them. It then stood by while the ducklings ate. When the ducklings were full, the gander ate what they had left and shepherded them back to the lake.

When ducks dive underwater for food, they tip forward, stretching their necks, leaving just their tail feathers poking above the water.

Ducks and geese

TOGETHER WITH SWANS, ducks and geese belong to the same family of waterfowl. They live on land and in water. Ducks differ from geese in that they have squatter bodies and shorter necks and legs, but neither ducks nor geese have legs well-suited to walking on land. Their legs are set very far back, which gives them their characteristic waddle.

WHEN IN WATER, ducks and geese are as balanced as rowing boats, using their broad, webbed feet as paddles to row themselves along. On the surface of the water, they look as if they are moving without effort, but underneath they are paddling furiously.

If you have ever seen a flock of migrating geese winging across the sky, a similar thing is happening in the air. Behind the

Geese migrate to winter feeding-grounds each year after the breeding season.

GANDERS ARE BELIEVED TO "TALK" TO GOSLINGS WHILE THEY ARE STILL IN THE EGG.

beauty of the V-formation is a lot of hard work, especially for the lead goose. It controls the speed of the flock, its direction, and its height from the ground. It is also the chief lookout and spots any danger ahead. Migrating geese and ducks fly in a V-formation because the air rushing past the leader gives an extra lift to others. Every bird in the group takes a turn at being leader.

When a gosling (baby goose) hatches, the first animal or thing it sees becomes imprinted in its memory. It regards the animal as its kin, and follows it everywhere. Viennese zoologist Konrad Lorenz found that his goslings adopted many things as their mothers, including a ball, a block of wood, and an Alsatian dog.

Swans

SWANS HAVE BEEN seen through the ages as symbols of purity, grace, and beauty, as well as loyalty, nobility, and courage. With their snowy white, curly feathers, long gracefully arched necks, and elegant wing spans, swans are truly graceful and beautiful birds. Riding high on the surface of a lake or river, swans glide serenely by, looking as if nothing in the world could trouble them.

Swan Upping

In England, U.K., swans on open and common water belong to either the Crown (the king or queen) or trade guilds. At one time, they all belonged to the Crown, but during the 15th century some of the swans on the River Thames were given to the trade guilds. Since then, all the swans that belong to the guilds are marked with a nick in the beak, while the Crown's swans are left unmarked.

Swan Song

A long-held belief is that swans sing just once before they die. Silent all their lives, their death song is said to be so haunting it would break the heart of the listener. Out of this, the phrase "swan song" has now developed, which means a person's last creative work.

Swans learn to fly at just three months old when they make their long migration south.

FLOCKS OF SWANS consist of separate families, each an adult pair, plus their fledglings (offspring.) Baby swans are called cygnets, and when born they are not white like their parents, but a dingy gray color. It takes some time for them to turn into recognizable swans. A female swan is called a pen, and a male swan, a cob. The loyalty and faithfulness of swans is both legendary and real—they mate with the same partner for the whole of their lives.

Swans can get angry if anything or anyone moves onto their territory. A sweep of a swan's

SWANS CAN FLY AT SPEEDS OF UP TO 50 MPH (80 KPH.)

a tempting target for the smaller birds to tease. Little grebes have been seen tweaking swans' tails and then diving beneath the water out of harm's reach. Once the swans have turned away, the grebes bob back up again to repeat the joke.

WHEN SWANS ARE ALARMED THEY STRETCH THEIR NECKS UPWARD.

wing is strong enough to break a human arm, and its beak can deliver quite a peck. Swans show tremendous courage when protecting their young and will attack anything they see as a threat.

Swans are very regal and dignified and this makes them

Penguin Adventure

A penguin was found asleep
on the doorstep of a house
by Wellington Harbour, North
Island, New Zealand. It was a
Fiordland penguin, usually
found off the coast of
South Island. Two attempts
were made to release it
on a beach 52 miles (84 km)
away. The first time it
climbed into the traveling
cage and went to sleep, the
second time it swam away,
but reappeared on the
Wellington Harbour doorstep
24 hours later. Finally the
penguin was flown south
in style and released into
its home waters.

*Penguins always seem a little
unsteady on their feet and
are often seen falling flat
on their round stomachs!*

Penguins

ENGUINS ARE SEEN as comedians of the bird
world, clowns in their movements and behavior.
Standing side by side in large groups, perfectly
still and upright, they can look like well-drilled
soldiers waiting for a command. Although they
are birds, penguins cannot fly and use their wings
to swim with great speed underwater, their short
legs with webbed feet acting as rudders.

PENGUINS SPEND much of their
time underwater, coming ashore
only to breed and molt. Their
feathers are short and glossy and
most importantly, waterproof.

Emperor penguins, the largest
of all the penguins, never actually
come to land, but gather on the
pack ice of the Antarctic seas.
Once a year,
the female
penguin

**THE RARE GALAPAGOS
PENGUIN, IS THE ONLY SPECIES TO
LIVE NEAR THE EQUATOR.**

lays one egg and then returns
to the water, while the male
incubates the egg on its feet
for 64 days.

Adélie penguins show true
grit when they make mammoth
migration treks across barren
ice to their Antarctic rookeries
(breeding grounds.) They have
been known to walk 500 miles
(805 km) or more in their slow,
awkward waddle. The males
watch over the eggs until they
hatch, then they walk another
97–160 miles (156–257 km)
to the sea to feed.

Pelicans

FOOD-CATCHING features strongly in the lives of pelicans. They are large, strong-flying birds that feed on fish, which they catch when swimming in shallow water or by diving from the air. The skin under their lower bills extends into a pouch, with which they trawl for fish. Food so dominates the lives of pelicans and their appetites are so huge, that they will even take fish from a human hand.

The Pelican's Beak

Many years ago on the islands of Fiji, lived a fisherman named Ratu Tatanga who wove the largest fish traps around. The pelican, who at that time could only catch one fish at a time in its thin beak, told Ratu of its plight. As a reward Ratu gave the pelican one of his fish traps to use as a beak so that the pelican could catch as many fish as possible in one scoop.

THE GREAT WHITE pelican is well-adapted for aquatic life. Its short, strong legs propel it in water and help its rather ungainly takeoff from the water's surface. Once up in the air, the long-winged pelican is a powerful flier and often travels with other pelicans in a spectacular V-formation group.

A pelican's pouch is simply

PELICANS EITHER LIVE NEAR THE COAST OR ON INLAND LAKES AND MARSHES.

a scoop. As it pushes its bill underwater, the pouch fills up with water and fish. On lifting its head, the pouch contracts, forcing out the water, and leaving just the fish.

Large numbers of pelicans breed together in colonies. The females lay two to four eggs in a nest of sticks and the young are cared for by both parents. A mother pelican, returning from a trip to the sea, regurgitates half-digested fish into her beak pouch, and the young dip at the food. They often tumble in head-first, legs kicking in the air, as they scrape for the bits at the bottom.

Brown pelicans are smallest

of all the pelicans and hunt differently from the rest. They catch fish by diving at top speed into the water from 50 ft (15 m) high. When they dive, they hold their wings back and curve their necks into S-shapes. Their necks have cushioning air sacs to take some of the impact of the plunge into the water.

Pelicans feeding habits are really quite extraordinary. One couple out fishing were joined by a hopeful pelican. They decided to feed it, having no idea of the huge quantities pelicans can eat. The bird ate and ate without pausing, until in the end it was so full it fell over!

A pelican's most dramatic and distinguishing feature is its huge pouch that hangs beneath its long, broad bill.

Pelicans and Christ

In Medieval times it was thought that as young pelicans grew, they often rebelled against the male bird and provoked its anger, so that it killed them. When the mother pelican returned to the nest, it pierced its own breast with its beak, and revived the young with its blood. Another belief was that the mother pelican fed them with its own blood. Christians linked this legend to Christ and the sacrifice he made for humankind, which is probably why many churches have pelicans in stained glass windows or carved on lecterns.

Seals

The Selkie

The Selkie are the mythical seal folk of the Orkney and Shetland Islands, just off the U.K. On land they appear in human form, but to travel through the sea they wear sealskins. A Selkie woman can be captured by the theft of her sealskin. The clan MacCodum of North Uist, in the Outer Hebrides, Scotland are known as "Silochd nan Ron," which translates as "the Offspring of the Seals."

The common seal has been known to make dives that last up to 30 minutes.

WITH THEIR LARGE, dreamy eyes, supple grace in water, and ability to look almost like a different animal on land, seals have long been linked with magical, shape-shifting powers. On land they have to drag themselves forward with their flippers, but in water they are highly skillful swimmers and divers and can stay in water for very long periods, diving to great depths.

A SEAL'S BODY IS TORPEDO SHAPED, WITH THICK LAYERS OF BLUBBER UNDER ITS SKIN.

Seal Sanctuary

Rescued, orphaned and injured seals often have to be taught to feed themselves, which is vital for them to survive in the wild. Large, an injured gray seal taken in by the Orkney Seal Rescue Centre, U.K., only ate fish when it thought no one was watching. When humans were around, it would only be hand-fed—probably hoping it could stay and eat "free food" in the sanctuary for a little bit longer!

IF YOU TRY SWIMMING underwater with your mouth open, you soon end up spluttering and swallowing water. A seal can close its nostrils while diving and strong muscles prevent water entering its throat when it opens its mouth underwater to feed. The flow of blood to heart muscle and brain is automatically slowed. This reduces oxygen use

THE WORD "SEAL" COMES FROM THE ANGLO-SAXON "SEOLB," MEANING "TO DRAG."

and allows the seal to stay underwater for longer.

The Weddell seals make deeper, longer dives than any other seals. They can hold their breath for 30 minutes, and dive to depths of 1,500 ft (457 m,) where the pressure would crush the hull of some boats.

The pups of bearded seals are born on the drifting ice floes of the Arctic and take to the sea almost at once. At less than a week old they can dive to 820 ft (250 m) and stay underwater for a period of five minutes.

Hippopotamuses

THE THIRD LARGEST LAND animals, found only in Africa, hippopotamuses were named by the ancient Greeks ("hippos" meaning "horse" and "potamos" meaning river) who thought that their cries sounded similar to the neighing of horses. Large and bulky, hippopotamuses are generally timid, but can be aggressive if disturbed. They are well-adapted to spend much of their lives in water.

Rerat

The hippopotamus was an important figure in ancient Egypt. The goddess Rerat, one of the keepers of the gates passed by the soul on its journey after death, was shown as a hippopotamus standing on hind legs. The goddess was a symbol of fertility, often figured pregnant and standing upright.

WHEN HIPPOPOTAMUSES are in water they lie with much of their vast bodies submerged, often with only their eyes, ears, and noses poking above the surface. They are able to close their nostrils when underwater, and secrete an oily substance which protects their bodies. They swim and dive well, and can walk on the bottom of a river or lake. When on land, they eat short grass and plants, and can reach speeds of up to 20 mph (32 kph.)

Baby hippopotamuses can swim within five minutes of being born, but to escape crocodiles and their not-too-gentle fathers, young hippopotamuses spend much time on their mothers' backs.

Hippopotamuses have a social etiquette about who stands where

THE PYGMY HIPPOPOTAMUS IS APPROXIMATELY HALF THE SIZE OF THE HIPPOPOTAMUS.

in the river. The female and the young stay in the center, while the males, each in his own patch, range along the edges. If a male wanders into a female's territory, he must lower himself into the water if she stands up. If he fails,

THE PYGMY HIPPOPOTAMUS IS EXTREMELY RARE AND IS EVEN EXTINCT IN SOME AREAS.

he will most likely be set upon by all the other females around. Male hippopotamuses can sometimes be bullies to the younger hippopotamuses, so this may be the reason females insist the males submerge themselves where they can do no harm.

The pygmy hippopotamus, as well as being much smaller than its giant relative, is much less aquatic. It lives near water, but stays on land for most of the time, feeding at night on leaves, swamp vegetation, and fallen fruit.

Rescue Attempt

A hippopotamus' amazing attempt to save a deer was caught on film, showing its bravery and defensiveness. The hippopotamus beat off a crocodile that was savaging a deer and made several attempts to lift the deer with its head. Finally it put its huge mouth over the deer's mouth in an attempt to resuscitate the poor animal. For all the hippopotamus' efforts, the deer died and the hippopotamus howled in anguish.

Hippopotamuses live in groups of up to 15 or so, led by an old male.

Ice Holes

Polar bears love to eat seals. A bear waits by the blow holes seals make in the ice, and then when a seal pops its head up to breathe some air, the bear grabs it. Sometimes a bear will stop up other breathing holes in the area to force the seals to use one particular blow hole and so increase its chances of catching a meal. One polar bear was even seen to throw handfuls of ice at a seal it missed!

Arctic Ancestors

One legend from the people of Lapland says that polar bears were thought to be ancestors of the Lapps, who called the bear grandfather. To the peoples of the northern lands, the polar bear was king of the beasts: swift, deadly, supremely powerful, and a killer of men. This may be because many of the Arctic peoples wear sealskins, rub seal oil on their bodies, and eat seal meat, and the polar bear, who likes seal meat, gets confused.

Little Bears

When born in November or December, polar bear cubs are around the size of a rat. They first see daylight, in March or April, and are then the size of a cat. The phrase "licked into shape," comes from the ancient belief that bear cubs were born as shapeless balls of fur, and the mother bear shaped them into baby bears with her tongue.

Polar bears

THE LONE WHITE HUNTER, found only in the Arctic, the polar bear wanders the white wastes of its icy world, king of this windswept and hostile environment. Equally at home on icy land and water, always on the move, and almost invisible with its white fur against the white landscape, the polar bear inspires both awe at its beauty, and fear of its power.

THE POLAR BEAR is nature's perfect stealth weapon. Almost invisible to the naked eye by day, it is truly invisible to modern night-vision glasses and even infrared cameras.

The fur of a polar bear is unique. It is a mass of hollow hairs, each with a smooth surface and a rough-coated core, which work in the same way as fiber-optics, with light entering each hair at its open end and bouncing

Polar bears have hairs on the soles of their feet to stop them slipping on the ice. When a polar bear gets too hot, it jumps into the sea to cool down.

POLAR BEARS ARE CONSTANTLY ON THE MOVE, TRAVELING AS FAR AS 75 MILES (120 KM) A WEEK.

down the hair tube until it reaches the bear's black skin at its root. Black absorbs more light and heat than other colors, perfect for a bear in a cold climate. Added to that, the hairs also let light in all the way round. These hairs also take in ultra-violet light and convert it to infrared light to heat the bear's body.

While the bear's hair is busily trapping warm light in the invisible part of the spectrum, it is also scattering most of the light in the visible part of the spectrum, giving it its whiteness. But that's not all the hairs can do! Running down the center of each is a central core of membranes that give the hair strength without

POLAR BEARS ARE THE LARGEST FLESH-EATERS ON LAND.

weight, so although the bear's coat is thick and warm, it is not too heavy. Added to that, in among the hairs are air pockets, a built-in life jacket that helps the bear float in the arctic seas.

Polar bears are one of the seven species of true bear, the only one to inhabit the Arctic regions.

A Warm Threat

Polar bears may be threatened by global warming. Arctic ice sheets have shrunk northwards in recent years, although whether this is due to global warming, or some other effect, is too soon to tell. Seals, the polar bear's favorite food, live and rear their young on the edge of these ice sheets. As their homes move northward, this takes the seals away from the rich waters where they normally find fish and krill on which to feed. If the seal numbers drop, then polar bears might struggle to survive.

CURIOUS CREATURES

Polar bears can be very curious and persistent in their interest. In 1969, a polar bear traveling on top of a ice-floe, drifted alongside a coastguard vessel in the Canadian Arctic. The crew fed it black molasses, jam, salami sausages, a jar of peanut butter, some salt pork, lots of chocolate bars, and an apple, which it spat out in disgust. When the food ran out, the bear climbed on board the ship. Not sure what to expect from a wild polar bear, the crew turned the water hoses on it. Big mistake! The polar bear loved that even better than the food, and even held its arms up for the crew to hose underneath!

Strong Swimmers

An excellent swimmer, the polar bear jumps into the water like a dog, or slides in backward. It can stay underwater for two minutes at a time, and using only its front legs, it cruises at about 6 mph (10 kph.) Polar bears have been seen 49 miles (80 km) from land or ice floes, and one was spotted swimming as far away as 200 miles (322 km) north of Greenland.

Otters

Floating Beds

Just under the ocean surface, kelp leaves spread out like a mattress, while deep below the roots are anchored in sand and rocks. When sea otters prepare for bed, they grab floating ends of sea kelp and roll over and over, wrapping themselves in the strands. Safely the otters sleep, pups in their mother's arms, while the kelp keeps them from drifting away during the night.

Even adult otters are playful— they enjoy sliding down muddy banks and rushing about.

SMALL ANIMALS with great hearts, otters are wild animals that happily live with humans, retaining their wildness, but giving and needing great affection and loyalty. They have a natural, joyful curiosity and from this spirit of delight in living, the otter brings the gift of play to humankind. Otters are endlessly curious about the world, and take great delight in exploring and trying something new.

OTTERS LIVE MAINLY along rivers and sea coasts, and in both environments, fish and eels are their main source of food.

The river otter has a long, slender body, covered in brown fur that is paler on its front and belly, small ears, a long, thick tail, and webbed feet. Its large, black feet act as flippers. The river otter averages 35–47 in (90–120 cm) in length and has a tail 15 in

BABY OTTERS HAVE TO BE TAUGHT HOW TO SWIM BY THEIR PARENTS.

(40 cm) long. River otters live in a holt or den in the river bank and are most active at night. They need clean rivers with a good fish supply and each otter may well range over 6 miles (10 km.)

The sea otter is around 39 in (1 m) in length with a tail 10–15 in (25-37 cm) long, and dense, dark brown, silky fur which traps an insulating layer of air to keep the animal warm.

Beavers

SHINING LIGHTS of the animal world, beavers are sociable, peaceful, hard-working, and faithful. They live in close-knit families and are master home-builders. Beavers lead semi-aquatic lives and are excellent swimmers. They are always found near waterways surrounded by dense woodland and feed on the bark and twigs from trees. They also use the wood to build their complex dams and lodges.

Timber!

A beaver is a small creature, standing about 2 ft (50 cm) high on its hind legs, yet it can bring down a tall tree using only its teeth. It chews around the tree trunk until most of the tree is balanced on a fine point off-center. It then waits for the tree to fall.

BEFORE THEY START to raise a family, male and female beavers find a stream and create their own pond by felling trees with their sharp teeth. Their dams are made of logs, piled up horizontally from the river bed, and held down and sandwiched together with layers of mud and stones. It is not unusual for a dam to be 330 ft (100 m) long, 16 ft (5 m) wide at the bottom, 5 ft (1.5 m) wide at the top, and 10–12 ft (3–3.5 m) high.

Once the dam is in place, beavers set to and build their home, or lodge. This is built rather like an Indian teepee, with one or two underwater entrances, an internal platform just above water level, and a roof of heavily woven thatch plastered with mud, which sets firm and keeps out intruders.

BEAVERS HAVE WEBBED FEET, AND FLAT TAILS THAT THEY USE AS RUDDERS WHEN SWIMMING.

It takes a pair of beavers about six months to build a lodge if they are taking their time, but if rushed they can do it in a month.

From their pond, the

A beaver's favorite foods are aspen and poplar bark. Its teeth keep growing until it dies, so a beaver must keep chewing to wear them down.

IF A BEAVER LOSES A TOOTH, IT WILL USUALLY DIE.

beavers then build a network of small canals to reach the trees on which the whole family feeds. Branches are ferried back to the lodge and stuck upright in the mud at the bottom of the pond. Come winter, the lodge is quite well-stocked.

Beavers are well-adapted for their aquatic habits. Their dense fur provides both waterproofing and insulation and their ears and nostrils can be closed off, allowing them to stay underwater for up to 15 minutes at a time.

The Beaver's Tail

Long ago, fire spread across the forest in which all the animals lived. The beaver called the river folk together, and they built a dam to flood the path of the fire. All the animals jumped for safety into the water, but a burning tree fell across the beaver's beautiful bushy tail. Luckily the beaver was pulled to safety, but its lovely tail was flattened and burned, and has been hairless ever since.

Weird and wonderful

W HILST MOST PREHISTORIC creatures are
long gone, some are still with us. Snow
fleas, some spiders, snails, cockroaches, and
the horseshoe crab have remained unchanged
for millions of years. Also on our planet are
many creatures that to our eyes look odd,
yet they are living evidence of the
wonderful variety of nature.

Cassowary

This large, black-feathered, flightless
bird is the only bird in the world
to have armor. It has a gray,
bony "helmet" on its
blue-skinned head.

Opossum

Nicknamed "Old Slowpoke," the opossum's
favorite trick is pretending to be dead if
attacked. This act is so convincing that even
a pack of hounds have been seen to give
up and go away, leaving the opossum
to get up and wander off.

Coelacanth

In 1938, a trawler fishing off the coast of
Africa caught a very odd-looking fish. It was
about 5 ft (1.5 m) long, steel-blue, and covered
in heavy scales. Until then scientists thought
the coelacanth, had died out more
than 65 million years ago.

Aardvark

Its name meaning "earth-pig" in African, this hump-backed, rabbit-eared, long-snouted animal feeds on ants and termites in many parts of Africa. Unlike the anteater, which is toothless, the aardvark has 20, rootless teeth which grow continually throughout its life.

Okapi

The okapi lives in the tropical forests of Central Africa. It has the legs of a zebra, the body of an antelope, and moves like a giraffe with the high speed of an ostrich. It also has four stomachs, eyes that can look in different directions simultaneously, and a transparent tongue 14 in (35 cm) long.

Duck-billed platypus

When scientists were first presented with the dead body of a duck-billed platypus, they thought someone was playing a joke on them. It looked as if bits of other animals had been stuck together. An egg-laying mammal that is at home in the water, the platypus is covered in fur with a beaver-like tail, has webbed feet and the beak of a duck. This oddity of nature has survived on the planet for 50 million years.

Tapir

A tapir looks as if it can't make up its mind whether it wants to be a pig, an elephant, or a rhinoceros. As a hoofed animal, it walks on its toes. However, its feet are unusual in that although each front foot has four toes, the hind feet have only three. A tapir can hide underwater using its trunk as a snorkel.

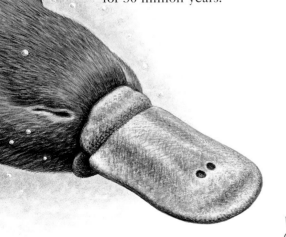

When diving underwater the duck-billed platypus uses its sensitive bill to probe for food.

Animals and superstitions

SUPERSTITIONS ARE BELIEFS that everyday objects, events, or signs have meaning or power. Centuries ago, people needed explanations for the unexplainable things, and animals, with their different appearance and behavior, were sometimes thought to be the causes of these events. Some superstitions were based on misunderstandings of observed animal behavior. For example, dogs often howl when a family member dies, so it was believed that if a dog howled continually, someone in the house was going to die.

Weather check

One superstition was that you could forecast the weather by watching a cat. If it washed behind its ears, rain was on the way. If it sat with its back to the fire, it was to be a frosty night. If it rushed about wildly, its ears pointing backward, then the wind was about to rise.

A cat's life

The animal most widely linked with superstition is the black cat. One old Norse legend tells the story of Freya, a Norse goddess who rode a chariot pulled by black cats. The cats served Freya faithfully, and as a reward, after seven years they were turned into witches. This tale led to the superstition that all cats were the familiars of witches, and that every black cat was, in fact, a witch in disguise.

There were other black cat superstitions. In Europe, if a black cat crossed your path, it was thought to be unlucky. If it walked toward you, it brought good luck, but if it walked away from you, your luck was on its way out! One belief common to all countries was that cats had special gifts. They were believed to foretell the future, and see spirits that humans could not. For this reason black cats were often kept aboard ships as lucky mascots. Even today, if a ship is going down, attempts will be made to save the cat along with the crew.

Freya and her black cats ride through the night.

Strange beliefs

Below are a few old superstitions that you may have heard before. Read the rest of this page and you will learn lots more.

- When you see a magpie, don't look away until you have seen its mate.
- Say, "White rabbits, black rabbits," on the first day of each month.
- Notice that when cows are lying down in a field, rain is on the way.
- When a ladybug lands on your hand, repeat the rhyme, "Ladybug, ladybug, fly away home. Your house is on fire and your children are gone."

Pigs

Pigs are supposed to be able to smell the wind. So, if a pig was seen running about with straw in its mouth, windy weather was thought to be on the way. Fishermen were very superstitious about pigs and would never say the word out loud.

Ants

It was believed that when ants were busy, bad weather was on the way. In Cornwall, U.K., ants were once thought to be fairies in the last stages of their existence on Earth. They were thought to have gone through changes that made them smaller and smaller until they disappeared altogether.

White horses

White horses were seen as both lucky and unlucky. In Great Britain, it was the custom to spit on the ground or make the sign of the cross with your foot, on seeing a white horse. However, in some areas it was thought to be lucky to lead a white horse through the house.

Magpies

Magpies were said to be lucky or unlucky, depending on how many were spotted!

"One for sorrow, two for joy, three for a letter, and four for a boy. Five for silver, six for gold, and seven for a secret never told."

Swans

The ancient Greeks and the Vikings linked swans to the gods, and thought they drew chariots across the sky. Swans mate with the same partner for life, so a swan's feather, sewn into a groom's pillow by his bride, was said to enlist the help of the gods and make sure the groom remained faithful.

Hens

If a hen went to roost at an unusual time, especially in the morning, it foretold a death in the family. A hen that crew like a cock, was supposedly bewitched, and therefore a very bad omen.

Beetle

Black beetles were once used as a cure for whooping cough. First a beetle was caught and put into a small box. This was then hung round the patient's neck. As the poor beetle starved and died inside the box, so the whooping cough gradually disappeared!

Spiders

Killing a spider was said to bring bad luck. A Bible story tells of when the Holy Family of Mary, Joseph, and their child Jesus, being chased by soldiers, fled into Egypt. Here, they hid in a cave. A spider wove a web across the entrance. When soldiers saw the web, they assumed the cave must be empty and passed by.

Kingfishers

A kingfisher's feather, especially a blue one, was said to protect you from stormy weather. This superstition was born from the inaccurate belief that kingfishers nested on water, and that the female used magic to calm the waves.

Bears

In Europe, bears were once a common sight at country fairs. Farmers thought that if a cow lost its calf, or a sheep its lamb, a bear was living nearby. This superstition probably originated because people believed that bears only bred every seven years. When they did, they brought bad luck to other breeding animals close by.

Snakes alive!

At Chiang Mai, Thailand, there is a special type of zoo called an open zoo. This means that many of the animals can wander around freely. Within the zoo there is a snake sanctuary. In October 1993, one of the snakes took a dislike to another snake, and a fight broke out. Thousands of snakes were involved, including many poisonous ones. It was impossible for keepers to separate them. There are many superstitions about snakes in Thailand, and the fight was seen as a bad omen. One Buddhist monk told journalists that in ancient times it would have meant that the country was about to be invaded by enemies.

Astrological animals

ASTROLOGY IS THE ancient art of studying the effect of the positions and movements of the planets on events on Earth. Astrologers believe that when a person is born, the position of the Sun, Moon, and the planets affects the character and abilities of that person and, therefore, their destiny (future.)

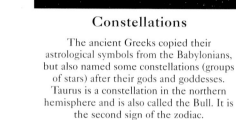

Constellations

The ancient Greeks copied their astrological symbols from the Babylonians, but also named some constellations (groups of stars) after their gods and goddesses. Taurus is a constellation in the northern hemisphere and is also called the Bull. It is the second sign of the zodiac.

Signs of the zodiac

In western astrology, a year is divided into twelve sections, or signs, which represent the journey of the stars across our night sky. Some signs are named after animals, and whichever one you are born under, you are supposed to share that animal's characteristics.

Capricorn
December 22–January 20
The goat is hard-working and has a need to succeed. It is cautious and resists change.

Aquarius
January 21–February 18
The water-carrier has strong, unconventional opinions and can stand alone.

Sagittarius
November 23–December 21
The archer likes change and travel. He loves to learn and dislikes routine.

Pisces
February 19–March 20
The fish is slippery and changeable, passionate, intuitive, and kind. It is also creative and imaginative.

Scorpio
October 24–November 22
The scorpion is loyal and private. It likes mysteries and is intense and passionate.

Aries
March 21–April 20
The ram is assertive, courageous, and enthusiastic.

Libra
September 23–October 23
The scales achieve balance and harmony. They dislike arguments and injustice.

Taurus
April 21–May 21
The bull is practical and reliable, but stubborn. It often has a beautiful voice.

Virgo
August 24–September 22
The maiden is private and preoccupied with health. She is cautious and likes to plan.

Gemini
May 22–June 21
The twins are changeable, like two people. They are adaptable and quick-thinking.

Leo
July 23–August 23
The lion is warm-hearted and generous. It is dramatic and has a powerful personality. It is also proud and loyal.

Cancer
June 22–July 22
The crab is a home- and family-lover. It is sensitive and retreats into its shell if upset.

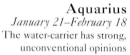

Chinese horoscopes

The Chinese system of astrology is based on the year in which a person is born. Each of the 12 segments is made up of 12 years, and each is represented by an animal.

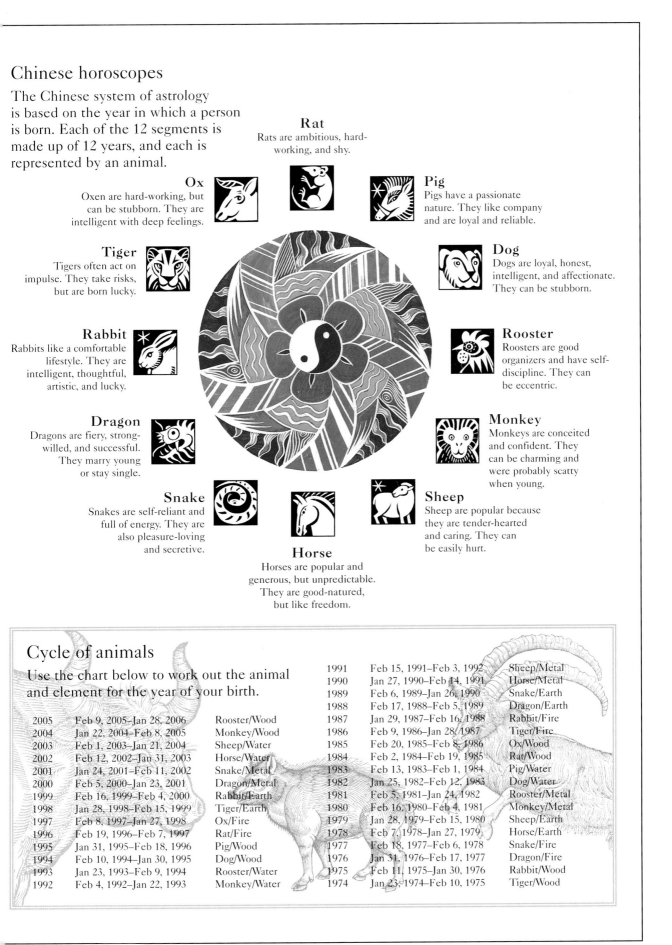

Rat
Rats are ambitious, hard-working, and shy.

Ox
Oxen are hard-working, but can be stubborn. They are intelligent with deep feelings.

Pig
Pigs have a passionate nature. They like company and are loyal and reliable.

Tiger
Tigers often act on impulse. They take risks, but are born lucky.

Dog
Dogs are loyal, honest, intelligent, and affectionate. They can be stubborn.

Rabbit
Rabbits like a comfortable lifestyle. They are intelligent, thoughtful, artistic, and lucky.

Rooster
Roosters are good organizers and have self-discipline. They can be eccentric.

Dragon
Dragons are fiery, strong-willed, and successful. They marry young or stay single.

Monkey
Monkeys are conceited and confident. They can be charming and were probably scatty when young.

Snake
Snakes are self-reliant and full of energy. They are also pleasure-loving and secretive.

Sheep
Sheep are popular because they are tender-hearted and caring. They can be easily hurt.

Horse
Horses are popular and generous, but unpredictable. They are good-natured, but like freedom.

Cycle of animals

Use the chart below to work out the animal and element for the year of your birth.

Year	Dates	Animal/Element
2005	Feb 9, 2005–Jan 28, 2006	Rooster/Wood
2004	Jan 22, 2004–Feb 8, 2005	Monkey/Wood
2003	Feb 1, 2003–Jan 21, 2004	Sheep/Water
2002	Feb 12, 2002–Jan 31, 2003	Horse/Water
2001	Jan 24, 2001–Feb 11, 2002	Snake/Metal
2000	Feb 5, 2000–Jan 23, 2001	Dragon/Metal
1999	Feb 16, 1999–Feb 4, 2000	Rabbit/Earth
1998	Jan 28, 1998–Feb 15, 1999	Tiger/Earth
1997	Feb 8, 1997–Jan 27, 1998	Ox/Fire
1996	Feb 19, 1996–Feb 7, 1997	Rat/Fire
1995	Jan 31, 1995–Feb 18, 1996	Pig/Wood
1994	Feb 10, 1994–Jan 30, 1995	Dog/Wood
1993	Jan 23, 1993–Feb 9, 1994	Rooster/Water
1992	Feb 4, 1992–Jan 22, 1993	Monkey/Water
1991	Feb 15, 1991–Feb 3, 1992	Sheep/Metal
1990	Jan 27, 1990–Feb 14, 1991	Horse/Metal
1989	Feb 6, 1989–Jan 26, 1990	Snake/Earth
1988	Feb 17, 1988–Feb 5, 1989	Dragon/Earth
1987	Jan 29, 1987–Feb 16, 1988	Rabbit/Fire
1986	Feb 9, 1986–Jan 28, 1987	Tiger/Fire
1985	Feb 20, 1985–Feb 8, 1986	Ox/Wood
1984	Feb 2, 1984–Feb 19, 1985	Rat/Wood
1983	Feb 13, 1983–Feb 1, 1984	Pig/Water
1982	Jan 25, 1982–Feb 12, 1983	Dog/Water
1981	Feb 5, 1981–Jan 24, 1982	Rooster/Metal
1980	Feb 16, 1980–Feb 4, 1981	Monkey/Metal
1979	Jan 28, 1979–Feb 15, 1980	Sheep/Earth
1978	Feb 7, 1978–Jan 27, 1979	Horse/Earth
1977	Feb 18, 1977–Feb 6, 1978	Snake/Fire
1976	Jan 31, 1976–Feb 17, 1977	Dragon/Fire
1975	Feb 11, 1975–Jan 30, 1976	Rabbit/Wood
1974	Jan 23, 1974–Feb 10, 1975	Tiger/Wood

Myth

● ● ● ● ● ● ● ● ● ● ● ● ● ● ● ● ● ●

Long ago, before we had films, computers, televisions, and books, people gathered around fires and told each other stories. Some were attempts to explain things people didn't understand, such as traits and characteristics they saw in the animals around them. Bigger myths explained how life and the world was created, why the seasons change, and how humankind first appeared on Earth. These myths often contained animals, because animals were very much part of life. So animals became symbols that helped us understand our world.

MANY MYTHOLOGICAL ANIMALS ARE BASED ON REAL ANIMALS WITH HUMAN EXAGGERATIONS.

YOUR VIEW OF LIFE AND THE DREAMS YOU HOLD INSIDE ARE YOUR PERSONAL MYTHOLOGY.

MYTHS ABOUT ANIMALS GROW FROM OUR NEED TO UNDERSTAND THE MYSTERY OF THEIR BEINGS.

Garuda

Garuda is one of the oldest mythical birds. It had a human body with an eagle's head, wings, and feet, and was the divine bird of India. It was called the "bird of life." Garuda was the enemy of all serpents that were thought to be evil, and made sure it ate a snake daily. It was so large that when flying, it blotted out the Sun. Garuda's face was white, its body golden, and its wings scarlet.

The Roc

In Arab folklore, the roc was such a huge bird it could carry an elephant in its talons. No one has ever properly described the roc, as it was so large it was impossible to see all of it at any one time.

However, the roc was supposed to have two horns on its head and four humps on its back. The Venetian explorer Marco Polo wrote about the rocs that lived on Madagascar.

Harpy

Harpies were foul-smelling, monstrous creatures with the heads of old women on the bodies of birds. Their feathers could not be damaged, and they flew with the speed of the wind. The name harpy means "snatcher" and the ancient Greeks thought that harpies were spirits of the wind who snatched up those mortals that the gods wished to see disappear, and carried them to the Underworld.

Mythical birds

BIRDS DO THE one thing humans cannot— they fly. In ancient times, the sky was the source of much that was unknown and uncontrollable—lightning, rain, wind, hail, and snow. Birds, who flew and survived in that environment, became creatures with superior powers—messengers of the gods, or even gods themselves.

ONE OF THE most magical of birds was the phoenix, or phenix, a mystical bird who lived alone for 500 years. It then sang its final song before burning itself in a specially built nest, set alight by the Sun's rays. From the ashes of the burned phoenix came a worm, which grew into another phoenix.

Because the phoenix was immortal and never died, it was

thought that there was always a phoenix somewhere in the world, although only one at a time.

Huge birds are part of Native American mythology, especially the thunderbird. Many, many years ago, when the world was young, two

The phoenix was a mythical Egyptian bird, said to live in a sacred wood in paradise.

Passamaquoddy Indians set out to find where thunder came from. They journeyed to two high mountains, which were constantly moving together and then apart. The first warrior leapt through the gap, but the second was caught and squashed. The first one continued and saw a

THE HO-OO IS THE JAPANESE PHOENIX. THE HO IS THE MALE, AND THE OO IS THE FEMALE.

camp of large wigwams on the plain below him. From inside the wigwams came men with wings, who flew away over the mountains. This was the home of the thunderbirds.

The ziz was not a loud snore, but an enormous, ancient bird that ruled all other birds. With its huge wings, the ziz protected smaller birds from harm and the Earth from the storms that blew from the south. Its eggs were so huge that when one accidentally fell to the Earth, its contents flooded six cities.

Thunderbird

Storms were supposedly caused when the thunderbird broke through the clouds, clapping its huge wings. Once a comanche warrior shot a huge bird. As it crashed to the ground, the warrior feared he had shot down the thunderbird. Suddenly a storm brewed up and the hunter was killed by a bolt of lightning.

Caladmus

Caladmus was a supernatural bird that appeared in the Middle Ages. It turned up at the bedside of the seriously ill and perched on the end of their beds. If Caladmus looked at the patients they would recover, but if it looked away from them they would die.

BIG BIRD

Marlon Lowe was just ten years old when his red hair turned white. Playing in his garden in Illinois, U.S., one day in July 1977, Marlon was snatched from the ground by a huge, black bird with a white ring on its neck. The bird rose into the air, the screaming boy dangling from its talons. Written accounts logged the bird as at least 4.5 ft (1.3 m) tall, with a wingspan of 8 ft (2.5 m,) and a hooked bill 8 in (45 cm) long. Fortunately for Marlon, his mother was nearby. She rushed at the bird, screaming and yelling so loudly that the bird dropped her son and flew off. The very next day Marlon's red hair turned white and he was afraid to go out for months.

Famous Dragon

Legend has it that on Dragon's Hill in Berkshire, England, U.K., a brave knight killed a fire-breathing dragon to save a maiden from being the dragon's next sacrificial victim. To this day, there is still a bare patch on Dragon's Hill, where it is said nothing will grow because the dragon's blood was spilled there. The knight became Saint George, patron saint of England.

Constellation

In Greek mythology, the hundred-headed dragon, Draco, guarded the magical garden of the golden apples of Hesperides. The hero of the tale, Hercules, was set the task of stealing the apples from the dragon's orchard. Hercules threw his spear at Draco, killing him immediately. A reward for his previous services Juno, one of the Greek gods, placed Draco in the heavens where he is now a constellation.

Dragon Ships

In the early days of sea travel, figureheads were carved on ships to give protection to the crew and "eyes" for the ship to find its way across the seas. Many different animals were used, but in northern Europe dragons or serpents were preferred. The Vikings were famous for their dragon-headed warships or "Serpents of the Sea."

Dragons

SAY THE WORD "DRAGON" and immediately people have a mental picture of what they think one looks like. Eastern or western, all dragons are magical creatures that have a knowledge of the ancient lore of the land. Dragons are thought to be wise and patient, but are also creatures whose fierceness is not to be treated lightly.

IN HER BOOK "*TEHANU*," Ursula le Guin describes how the great dragon Kalessin, a powerful and ancient creature who lives beyond the rim of the world, comes to the aid of two humans. As Kalessin approaches, the humans stand on a cliff top. They tell of the roar of fire that passes over them, the rattle of the scaly armor, the hiss of the wind in its wings, and finally, the clash of talons as it lands on the rock. A dragon does not arrive quietly!

Dragons of western myth and

THE FIRST MAP-MAKERS WROTE "HERE THERE BE DRAGONS" ON UNEXPLORED LANDS.

legend take all forms, from serpents with wings, to huge, reptilian monsters with scaly bodies, wings that could lift a small coach from the ground, and fiery breath.

Western legends often show the dragon as a monster that needs to be killed to restore good. Sometimes western dragons are said to hoard huge piles of treasure or terrorize

CHINESE DRAGONS ARE CALLED "LUNGS" AND ARE CONSIDERED DIVINE, LIKE ANGELS.

whole villages full of people. Dragons from the East are often wingless, more gentle, and likely to give humans gifts or bring good luck.

The dragon has been worshiped at some time or another by almost every race in the world.

Throughout history, dragons have tended to be green, red, gold, and black. However, Chinese and other eastern dragons are more colorful and the hues have meanings, for example—yellow for luck, black for destruction, and azure for an important birth. Eastern dragons can also change from the size of a tiny caterpillar, to the huge expanse of the Universe in a second. They speak in delicate, tinkly voices and rest quietly under the sea or underground.

Welsh Flag

For centuries, the red dragon was the national symbol displayed on the war standard of the ancient Britons and the Welsh. The symbol is linked to King Arthur who dreamed that the green Saxon dragon fought the red dragon of the Britons, and the red dragon won. Today, the Welsh national flag still features a red dragon.

Dragon Dance

In China, the dragon represents cleverness, good fortune, and nobility. The dance of the dragon is used to drive out devils and bring good luck to the community. This dance became popular during the Sung dynasty (A.D. 960–1279,) and today, around 1,000 years later, the colorful dragon dance is still performed at Chinese festivals. At least twelve dancers, one drummer, and one leader are needed for the dance. One team performs with a golden dragon 394 ft (120 m) long.

Lion and Unicorn

Ever since 1603, the British royal arms have been supported by the English lion and the Scottish unicorn. The lion and the unicorn in the rhyme symbolized the fight between England and Scotland for the throne of England:

"The lion and the unicorn
were fighting for the crown,
The lion beat the unicorn
all around the town.
Some gave them white bread
and some gave them brown,
And some gave them plum
cake and drummed them
out of town."

Hippogriff

In Greek mythology, the hippogriff existed in the Riphaean mountains of Europe. It was a winged horse with an eagle's head and claws. The Moorish hero Rogero escaped from prison on the back of a hippogriff that his wife Bradamante, had won from an enchanter.

Magical horses

THERE ARE MANY different types of mythical horses and perhaps because of the sense of freedom horses have, most of them were born from dreams and desires, rather than from fears. This is certainly true of the unicorn, which with its beauty, pure white coat, and magical horn, promotes gentleness and selfless love. Pegasus, the winged horse, represents the carrier of dreams, and can gallop high above the Earth to the realms of myth and poetry.

THERE HAS BEEN MUCH debate over the centuries as to whether the unicorn was a purely mythical or real beast. If it was real, it has certainly disappeared from Earth

ALEXANDER THE GREAT WAS TAUGHT MANY SKILLS BY THE CENTAUR CHIRON.

The unicorn was believed to become calm in the presence of young maidens.

today. The unicorn was first described by the Greek historian Ctesias in 398 B.C. Ctesias was a doctor who worked at the court of the Emperor of Persia, so had probably heard of many interesting sights and tales from travelers. He described the unicorn as having a white body, a dark red head, and deep blue eyes, and claimed that it was, "exceedingly swift and powerful and no creature, neither the horse or any other, could overtake it."

China's unicorn, the K'I-lin, had a multicolored body and a horn 12 ft (3.7 m) long. Its voice was said to sound like a thousand wind chimes, and it walked so softly its hooves made no sound.

The fierce Muslim unicorn, the Kar-ka-dann, was more like a cow or a bull than a horse. The Kar-ka-dann was so noisy, the only thing that could quieten it was the cooing of a dove.

Only since the Middle Ages has the unicorn become more

THE ADH SIDHE ARE IRISH FAERIE CREATURES WHO APPEAR AS BLACK HORSES.

Pegasus gallops through the sky, flapping his magnificent wings.

horse-like, and in Europe it is now seen as a white horse with a flowing mane. Although hard to find and gentle by nature, the unicorn was renowned as a fierce fighter. The recommended way to catch a unicorn was to stand in front of a tree with a large trunk, and taunt the unicorn until it charged. The hunter would then step aside exposing the trunk to the unicorn's sharp horn.

The other famous magical horse is Pegasus, the amazing flying horse from Greek mythology. When the Greek hero Perseus killed the snake-haired Gorgon by cutting off her head, blood soaked into the ground. It was from this blood that Pegasus grew. The goddess Minerva tamed him and finally gave him to the Muses who lived on Mount Helicon.

At one time, the Muses held a song contest and the music was so powerful, Mount Helicon started to grow toward heaven. Unhappy about this, the god Poseidon asked Pegasus to strike the mountain with his hoof to make it stop growing. Pegasus struck the rock, and the Hippocrene fountain started to flow. From that day, its waters have inspired poets.

A UNICORN'S HORN IS CALLED AN ALICORN.

Centaurs

Centaurs were beings that had the body of a man to the waist, and the body and legs of a horse from the waist down. In Greek mythology, centaurs lived in Thessaly, but the earliest known tales of them come from Babylon around 2000 B.C. The Kassites moved to Babylon in 1750 B.C. and took with them drawings of centaurs with wings and two tails.

Sleipnir

Sleipnir was an eight-legged horse belonging to Odin, the Norse god of war. Swifter than all horses, no obstacle was too great for Sleipnir, who could gallop across both land and sea. His father was Svadlifari, a giant's horse and his mother was Loki, a Norse god who had changed himself into a mare. Sleipnir once trod on Iceland, and the mark of his hoof can be seen today at Asburgi in northeast Iceland.

Mami Wata

Mami Wata is a mermaid water spirit that lives in the waters of western and central Africa. She has long, dark hair, hypnotic eyes, and very fair skin. It is said she also walks the streets of Africa disguised as a woman.

Mermaid of Zennor

As everyone knows, mermaids are supposed to have beautiful voices and love to sing. In the village of Zennor, in Cornwall, U.K., there once lived a young man with a voice like a clear, sweet bell. Down in the cove, a mermaid heard his song and fell in love with him. The young man went to live with her under the sea where they sang beautiful songs together. It is said that in listening to his songs, the fishermen of Zennor knew when it was safe to put to sea, and when they should turn for home and a safe harbor.

Triton

In Greek mythology, Triton was the son of the god Poseidon and the sea-goddess Amphitrite. Some tales call him the god of seafarers and say he fathered a whole race of tritons. Nearly all the images of him show him blowing a conch shell. In 1960, the American submarine, the U.S.S. Triton, was the first nuclear-powered submarine to sail around the world completely submerged.

Mermaids

MERMAID LEGENDS are as old as the world's oldest cultures. Always beautiful, usually unhappy, mermaids are women to their waists, and below they have a scaly fishtail. A mermaid is often pictured sitting on a rock, looking into a mirror and combing her waist-length golden hair. Records of creatures half human, half fish go back as far as 1800 B.C.

TO THE PECH INDIANS of Honduras, U.S., the mother of all fish was a nine-eyed mermaid called Sirena. Before a fishing trip they would ask her permission to catch fish, as fishing without permission was thought to lead to illness or death.

Luxembourg, Germany, was

THE JAPANESE MERMAID "NMGYO" IS A FISH WITH A HUMAN HEAD.

founded by Count Siegfried, who had a beautiful young wife called Melusina. When Siegfried first asked her to marry him she agreed on one condition, that he

THE POLYNESIAN CREATOR-GOD IS HALF MAN, HALF PORPOISE.

would leave her alone for one full day each month. Because he loved her so much, Siegfried agreed. For many years, on the first Wednesday of every month, Melusina would go down to the casemates, a network of underground caverns beneath the city, and spend the day there. One day, Siegfried followed her and found her as a mermaid, lying in a tub full of water. The minute

THE IRISH CALL MERMAIDS "MERROWS" AND THE CORNISH CALL THEM "MERRYMAIDS."

she realized her secret had been found out, Melusina jumped from the window into the Alzette River and was never seen again.

Many places have tales of mermaids who have fallen in love with a human and chosen to live a lonely life on land away from their own folk. Some tell of human men who have fallen in love with a mermaid and trapped her by taking her "merskin" while she was dancing on a beach in human form.

Famous Mermaids

The Little Mermaid sits on a rock in the harbor of Copenhagen, Denmark. She was sculpted by Edvard Erikson in 1913 in memory of Hans Christian Anderson who wrote the story of "*The Little Mermaid*." In the story, the mermaid fell in love with a prince and the price she paid to become human and be near him was the loss of her beautiful voice. Sadly, this meant she could never tell him that she loved him.

Mermaids and mermen are said to be able to turn the sunniest of days into a storm.

A FISHING TALE

On April 20, 1814, the Aberdeen Chronicle, in the U.K., ran a report that two fishermen returning from Spey Bay, Scotland, were about a quarter of a mile (half a kilometer) offshore when they saw a man in the sea with his back to them. The fishermen rowed over to the man and had nearly reached him when he heard them coming and turned. His skin was a brownish color and his hair green-gray. He had a flat nose, small eyes, a large mouth, and very long arms. He was a man to the waist, but past the waist his body tapered into a fishtail. As the fishermen watched in astonishment, the man dived and resurfaced with a female, who also had a tail.

A Mermaid's Tears

On the Holy Island of Iona, off the coast of Scotland, U.K., are gray-green pebbles, said to be the tears of a mermaid who was in love with a saint who lived on the island. The mermaid visited the saint every day, but all he would tell her was that to gain a soul she must leave the sea. In despair she knew she could never do this. To this day, all that remains on the shore are the tears she cried.

Water creatures

Kraken

"Kraken" is an old Norse word for a terrifying, many-armed sea creature. Fishermen and sailors told tales of this monster whose back was so long—around 1 mile (1.6 km)—that sometimes it was mistaken for a floating island! Its great tentacles could easily reach the top of a sailing ship's mast, or wrap around a boat's hull and drag it to the bottom of the sea.

Kelpie

The kelpie is the waterhorse of Scottish rivers. Its close relation is the uisage, a waterhorse found in Scottish and Irish lochs and sea inlets of the U.K. Both of these creatures are unfriendly to humans. They look like docile horses, but if mounted, they rush off into the water and eat their riders. Once on a waterhorse, it is impossible to dismount. However, if a human manages to bridle a kelpie, it must obey his or her command.

Reported sightings of the Loch Ness monster go back as far as A.D. 6.

M OST COUNTRIES HAVE stories of mythical creatures that inhabit the seas, rivers, lakes, wells, and pools of the world. Earth's waters are so vast and deep, our imaginations have run wild. There have been many sightings of water monsters, but they are still a mystery. Although it is likely they are creatures of myth, built around sightings of swimming otters or large fish, there is always the possibility that some of these monstrous creatures might exist!

THE MOST FAMOUS of all water creatures are the lake monsters. Most countries have one. Scotland, U.K. has Nessie, the monster in Loch Ness. Lake monsters from the U.S. include Ogopogo, long, slim, and snake-

PING-FENG IS A CHINESE WATER MONSTER THAT LOOKS LIKE A BLACK PIG.

like with a whiskery, horse-like head in Okanagan Lake, British Columbia, Manipogo in Lake Manitoba, and Champ, also snake-like with the head of a horse, in Lake Champlain. If you want to see Bessie, you'll need to go to Lake Eerie, Canada, and look out for a snake-like

creature, 30–50 ft (9–15 m) long. Tessie lives in Lake Tahoe, U.S. It even has its own museum with a telephone hot-line for people to report sightings of it! Yuk, seen around the King Islands, British Columbia, usually only pokes its snake-like head and tail flipper out of the water.

China has Chan, a giant, vapor-breathing monster that lives in a lake in a deep gorge in a wild, mountainous area. Fishermen throwing dynamite into the lake to kill fish were chased by an annoyed Chan.

Lake Kos Kol, in Kazakhtan, Russia, also has a Loch Ness-type monster living in it.

In Patagonia, Nahuelito lives in the 318 square mile (824 km²) Nahuel Huapi Lake, at the foot of the Patagonian mountains. Many years ago the local Indians told tales of a giant water animal, and in 1922, scientists launched a search for a Patagonian plesiosaur (a dinosaur-like creature) after huge tracks were found around the edge of the lake.

At the end of 1995, Turkish investigators went to the country's largest lake, Lake Van, to look for another "Nessie." Reports said it was black and looked like a dinosaur with spikes on its back.

DEATHLY PUZZLE

In March 1969, the carcass of a strange sea creature was found on the beach in Tecoluta, Mexico. It weighed 35 tons (36 tonnes) and was covered in hard, jointed armor. Most puzzling of all was a tusk of bone, 10 ft (3 m) long, protruding from its head. A seven-man team of scientists commissioned to study the carcass, decided it might be a fin-back whale, but this still did not explain the huge tusk. Biologists who saw the carcase said they "could not match it with any sea creature known to man."

River Dragon's Pearl

All Chinese dragons have a magic pearl, a gem of great power, which they keep hidden—usually in the folds of their leathery chins or in the mud at the bottom of their lake or river. Anything the dragon touches with its pearl, grows and multiplies. Once, long ago, a poor Chinese boy planted some vegetable seeds in the river meadow where the grass was always lush and thick. As he dug he found a glowing ball. It was the river dragon's pearl. From then on, his fortune changed!

131

Once a beautiful Libyan queen called Lamia was loved by the god Jupiter and bore him children. The jealous goddess Juno stole the children. As Lamia could not harm the goddess, she turned herself into a serpent-woman and vowed to kill and eat any human child she came across. Since then it was thought that many lamias, descended from that first Lamia, lived in the deserts of Africa where the whistling sound they made lured travelers to their death.

Serpents

IN MANY RELIGIONS, serpents, or snakes, were worshiped as gods or used as symbols. Because they shed their skin and emerged with a new one, snakes were seen as symbols of new life and resurrection. In Christianity, the snake is mostly linked to the devil and death, although Moses, when his people were struck by a plague in the desert, lifted up a brass snake that had the power to heal all those who looked at it.

When one of the Hydra's heads was cut off, two more were said to grow in its place.

A COILED SNAKE, with its tail in its mouth, forms a circle, and so was often taken as a symbol for eternity—endless and limitless time. In old Norse legend, the Midgard serpent was thrown into the sea by Odin, where it grew so large it could encircle Earth and bite its own tail. It was often

BOAS WAS AN ENORMOUS SERPENT THAT LIVED IN ITALY IN A.D. 1.

thought that the serpent's thrashings in the sea caused storms.

In Hindu mythology, the god Vishnu rides a cobra, and sleeps on the coiled serpent of Earth's waters. The Celts linked the serpent to healing waters.

The Hydra was a many-headed serpent that lived in a swamp near the well of Amymone, in the country of Argos. If one of the heads of the Hydra was cut off,

ECHIDNA WAS THE HALF SERPENT MOTHER OF THE HYDRA IN GREEK MYTHOLOGY.

two more grew in its place. The head at the center was immortal, and one of the impossible tasks given to the Greek hero Hercules was to destroy the Hydra. He managed to burn away the side heads and buried the center head under a rock.

The Aido Hwendo was a giant rainbow serpent from ancient African mythology, who carried the creator goddess Mawn as she created the Universe. She then coiled beneath the Earth to support its weight. It was thought that when Aido Hwendo changed position, she caused an

AMPHISBAENA WAS A MEDIEVAL SERPENT WITH A HEAD AT EACH END OF ITS BODY.

earthquake.

For the Aborigines in Australia, the giant rainbow serpent in their mythology created life, but in China and Africa, the serpent was seen as a rain-maker and the rainbow serpent as a thirst-quenching god. Native Americans also link the snake with rain-making, and have rain-making dances in which they imitate the

movements of a snake.

Ancient Greek and Roman altars often had a serpent carved on them and pet snakes were kept to guard the home. One Roman guardian serpent was called a "genius."

Quetzalcoatl is one of the oldest and most important gods and rulers of ancient Mexico. He was the Toltec god of learning, knowledge, air, holiness, and self-sacrifice, and was known as the feathered serpent god—the plumed serpent, who went to the Underworld to collect bones, which he sprinkled with his own blood to make the human race.

Medusa

In Greek mythology, Medusa was a mortal woman who became one of the three Gorgons— terrible female monsters with wings, claws, and enormous teeth. Medusa's hair was a mass of writhing snakes and one glance at her face turned an onlooker to stone. She was killed by the hero Perseus, who cleverly avoided looking directly at her by using his shield as a mirror.

The Lambton Worm

During the Middle Ages, it was considered unlucky to fish on a Sunday. Young John Lambton did just that, and caught a strange worm in the River Wear, U.K., which he threw into a well and forgot about. Years later, when Lambton was a knight fighting in the crusades, the worm had grown into an enormous serpent that terrorized the countryside. When Sir Lambton returned from the Holy Land, he killed the worm, and restored the peace.

WHOA BOA!

On August 19, 1991, a black serpent, probably a boa constrictor, estimated to be the length of two passenger buses, 130 ft (40m) long and 15 ft (4.6 m) in diameter, crashed through the jungle undergrowth and terrified the villagers of Nevo Tacna, Peru. Reports on Peru's two national radio stations said the serpent had left a deep track wide enough to drive a tractor through, knocking down every tree in its path through the jungle and the village, before slipping into the River Napo. The incident was first reported by Jorge Chovez, Mayor of Mainas, 170 miles (274 km) north-east of Lima.

Chimera

The chimera is a female, fire-spewing monster from Greek mythology. It has a lion's body, a lion's and goat's head, and a dragon's tail. The chimera is often used to symbolize the impossible. The Greek hero Bellerophon killed the chimera with the help of the goddess Minerva and the winged horse Pegasus.

Salamander

In the Middle Ages, a salamander was a lizard-like spirit that could live in fire unharmed: its body was so cold it quenched the heat of the fire. King Francis I of France had a lizard surrounded by flames on his badge design, with the words, "*Nutrisco et extinguo*," which means, "I nourish and extinguish." Alchemists (early chemists) were rumored to use salamanders as temperature gauges when heating fire to turn lead into gold. When the fire was hot enough, the salamander leapt into the flames!

Cockatrice

The cockatrice and the basilisk both have the upper body of a rooster and the lower body of a snake, and are supposedly hatched by a snake from a cock's egg. Just one glance from a cockatrice was said to kill. Its bite and the touch of its tail was so poisonous that once when a rider on a horse killed a basilisk with a spear, the creature's venom rose through the spear and killed both horse and rider.

Fabulous beasts

MYTHS AND LEGENDS are full of fabulous creatures, many of whom had power over aspects of life or provided tests for heroes. The creatures represented many different ideas from sacred truths and the power of the forces of nature, to birth, death and rebirth, and the triumph of good over evil.

THE GRYPHON, or griffin was one of the noblest of the fabulous beasts. Made from two symbolically royal animals, it had the ears, body, hind legs, and tail of a lion and the head, forefeet and wings of an eagle. The gryphon combined knowledge, wisdom, strength, and honor.

THE GRYPHON WAS KNOWN TO THE SUMERIANS BY THE NAME OF CHUMBABA.

It was the link between man and the gods, being both beast and bird, of heaven and of Earth.

Stronger than eight lions and 100 eagles, the gryphon's size was so great it was said to block out the Sun when flying. Sometimes called the "Hounds of Zeus," gryphons were good guardians, showing great gentleness if guarding humans from harm, but fierce protectiveness when guarding treasure.

Gryphons were said to build their nests near buried treasure, or collect their own hoard. They were constantly at war with a race of one-eyed Sythian people, the Arimaspians, who were forever trying to steal their treasure.

The gryphon seems to have originated in Middle Eastern legends. The earliest known picture of one is carved on a seal found in what is now Iran and dates back to around 3000 B.C. In 7 B.C., the Greek writer Aristeas described gryphons that lived in a mountain range that could be the Urals or the Altai. By A.D. 14, gryphons were shown in Roman folklore drawing a chariot of the Sun across the sky. The Greek god Apollo also rode a gryphon, and they later became a common symbol

The gryphon is one of the most popular beasts in heraldry and appears on many coats of arms.

THE ART OF ANCIENT PERSIA CONTAINED MANY IMAGES OF GRYPHONS.

in heraldry. In legend gryphons also symbolized arrogant pride. This was because Alexander the Great once tried to ride on one to the edge of the sky.

Nemesis, the goddess of retribution, took the form of a gryphon at times, and it was a gryphon who turned her wheel of fortune. In ancient Roman art, gryphons drew the chariot of Nemesis. They were seen as avenging beasts, relentlessly pursuing anyone who upset them.

GRYPHONS BUILT NESTS AND LAID EGGS MADE OF AGATE—A GEMSTONE.

Kappa

The Kappa lives in rivers in Japan and is harmless if treated politely. It has the head of a monkey, the body of a tortoise, and the legs of a frog. On the top of its head is a depression filled with water, and from this water it gets its strength. If a Kappa attacks, the best way to defeat it is to bow, causing it to bow in response and so tip out the water on his head. It will then have to go back into the water for more. To avoid such meetings, carve your name on a cucumber and throw it into a river— the Kappa will then spare you!

QUESTING BEAST

In British folklore, the questing beast is an animal with a serpent's head, a leopard's body, and the hooves of a deer. It was also known as the "Beast Glatisant." The cry of the questing beast was said to be like the baying of 60 hounds and terrible to hear. In the tales of King Arthur and his knights of the Round Table, King Arthur first saw the beast in a dream. In the dream the only time the beast was quiet was when it was drinking. One of the knights, Pellinore, spent his life chasing the questing beast and at his death, the Saracen knight Palomides took over the Quest.

The Cyclopes

At the time when the heroes of old were returning to Greece after the Fall of Troy, the island of Sicily was believed to be inhabited by one-eyed giants, called Cyclopes. These giants had one enormous eye in the middle of their forehead. They were skillful shepherds who herded vast flocks of sheep on the mountains. Cyclopes fed on the flesh of sheep— and any people they could catch!

Werewolves

In Europe, in the late Middle Ages many men and some women were accused and convicted of being werewolves— humans who turned into hungry wolves at night. In France, between 1520 and 1630, more than 30,000 people were put on trial accused of being werewolves.

Genie

In Middle Eastern and Islamic folklore, a genie, or jinni, is a spirit made of fire or air, which can take on the form of a human or an animal. Genii are mischievous creatures, who enjoy annoying humans, which is why they are often blamed for accidents.

Satyrs and friends

MANY CREATURES of mythology belong neither entirely to the animal kingdom nor to the world of humans, being part man and part beast. Some of the most famous of these creatures were the satyrs, men with the horns, ears, and hindquarters of a goat. Generally they were seen as mischievous and idle, preferring to enjoy themselves rather than doing anything useful.

SATYRS WANDERED the wild places of the countryside. Companions of Dionysus, the god of wine, they spent their time drinking and dancing. The Romans called them fauns.

Pan was a satyr, he was the god of the woods, fields, flocks, and shepherds, and lived in the woods and mountains. A keen musician, he invented his own reed pipe, called the "syrinx" or "pan pipes." This happened when he was chasing a wood spirit, or nymph called Syrinx. She changed herself into a bed of reeds to escape Pan, and he pulled up some reeds and played a tune on them. Thereafter, he would play on his pipe while the woodland nymphs danced.

Pan dwelt in caves and dark places and walked softly in the wood at night. The sound of his distant music or his sudden appearance often frightened travelers, and so the word "panic" came to mean a

Satyrs are gods of the forest. They include pans, sylvans, and fauns.

PAN, THE SON OF HERMES, WAS MESSENGER OF THE GODS AND A NYMPH.

was drinking and dancing.
He was also seen as the
protector of cattle and was
often pictured holding a
goblet and wearing a wolf
skin. This is probably because
the Romans also sometimes
called him Lupercus, which
means "he who wards off
the wolf."

In Roman mythology,
Faunus became the king
of Latium in southern Italy.

**SOME SATYRS ONLY HAD ONE
EYE AND NO NOSE. THEY BREATHED
THROUGH THEIR CHESTS.**

He was the son of Picus,
the Roman god of agriculture,
and the grandson of the god
Saturn. His partner was Fauna,
the Roman earth mother and
fertility goddess. On February 15
each year, the people of ancient
Rome celebrated the Festival
of Lupercalia, to honor the
god Faunus. During the
festival the priests of Lupercus,
called Luperci, dressed in
goatskins and walked through
the streets of Rome amid
pagan celebration.

Were-Jaguars

The ancient Olmecs and
Mayans believed that
were-jaguars, beasts with
the head, body, and tail
of a jaguar and the legs
of a man, came from the
supernatural world to prey
on humans or teach them
lessons. In Mayan mythology,
four giant jaguar gods held up
the sky: a white one at
the north corner, a yellow
one at the south corner,
red at the east, and
black at the west.

Sirens

The sirens were water
creatures from ancient
Greek legends. Half
woman, half bird, they sang
enchanting songs to lure
sailors to their doom on
the rocks and reefs. In
ancient Greek mythology,
the hero Odysseus escaped
from the sirens by
plugging the ears of his
crew so they could not hear
the songs, and by having
himself tied to the
ship's mast so he could
not follow their
haunting sounds.

MINOTAUR

In ancient Greek mythology, the Minotaur
was the child of Queen Pasiphae of Crete, Greece, and
was a man with the head of a bull. His father Minos kept him
imprisoned in an underground maze that was so complicated, no
one could find their way out. The Minotaur ate only human flesh,
so Minos had arranged with the King of Athens that every nine
years, seven girls and seven boys were sent underground for
it to eat. One year, Theseus, the king's son was one of the
chosen children. With the help of Minos' daughter, who gave him
a ball of string to track his way round the maze, Theseus killed
the Minotaur and put an end to the human sacrifices.

sudden fright or terror without
any visible cause. His name also
means "all" and eventually Pan
came to be seen as a symbol of
the whole world of nature.

Faunus was the Roman god
of wild nature and, like the
satyrs, his favorite occupation

Ghostly animals

WHAT IS A GHOST? No one really knows, but the fact that there are many reports of them being seen means that they must fall within the laws that operate in our universe— we probably just don't know all of the laws yet! Some ghosts appear as solid and real, others seem unaware of their surroundings, and some are seen repeating the same action over and over again. Animals that have died, have often been reported as appearing as ghosts to warn someone they loved of danger.

Black dogs

There have long been reports that many areas of Britain and France are being haunted by a huge black, shaggy-coated dog with red eyes. Usually the dog appears and disappears silently, sometimes seeming to vanish into thin air near water or bridges over water, leaving a strong smell of sulphur behind.

Many sightings have occurred near ancient sites, such as long barrows, standing stones, old churchyards, or old tracks that follow ley lines. The dog looks real and solid, but often, if touched, it explodes or bursts into flames. In some accounts the dog is protective, in others it is threatening.

In 1577, a black dog suddenly appeared in the aisle of a church in Blythburgh, U.K. during the morning service. It attacked three people and burned another person. As it left the church, the dog scorched the door. These scorch marks can still be seen today. On the same day the dog appeared in the church at Bungay, seven miles from Blythburgh.

The ghostly vision of a black dog with red eyes has been seen haunting our countryside today.

Animal ghost stories

- Pond Square, London, U.K. is haunted by the ghost of a shivering, half-naked chicken that flaps round in circles. In Pond Square in 1626, Francis Bacon tried to freeze a chicken in snow.
- Cats and dogs that have died are said to return and haunt the steps outside the Church of San Giovanni Decollato, Rome.
- A stretch of road leading from Rathfarnham Castle, Ireland, is haunted by the ghost of a dog who tried to save his master from drowning.
- In August 1925, Major Wilmot Alistone took a photograph of his small son at Clarens, Switzerland. A few days earlier the child's small kitten had been killed by a St. Bernard dog. When the photograph was developed, a white kitten could be seen nestling in the boy's hands.
- Wild beasts were once kept caged in the underground passages of the Coliseum, Rome and it is said that in the fall of each year their ghosts return to haunt the site of their misery.
- White Horse Plain, Winnipeg, Canada, was named after the white horse given by a Cree chief in the 1690s for the hand of the daughter of another Cree chief. A jealous Sioux Chief killed the young couple and the white horse roamed the plain, first as a living horse and then as a ghost.
- In the early 19th century, Tennessee farmer, John Bell, and his family were haunted for four years by a snarling black dog and a strange bird bigger than a turkey.

The white horse

The ghost of an Englishman on a white horse is said to haunt the South African bush. In the late 1800s, this man was reported to have ridden into the bush and shot seven elephants. Later his horse returned without him. The Englishman was never found and by sunset the horse had died.

Photographic play

Images of a family pet may appear in a photograph taken long after the pet has died. Lady Hehir, a noblewoman from Ireland, once had two dogs, an Irish wolfhound called Tara, and a Cairn puppy called Kathal. Tara and Kathal were close friends, but sadly little Kathal died in 1927. About six weeks later a friend of Lady Hehir's photographed her standing by Tara. When the photograph was developed, little Kathal could be seen in the photograph too.

Extinct animals

EVERYONE KNOWS that dinosaurs are long gone and that dodos are dead, but do you know that since the 1600s at least 300 animal species have become extinct. Many more will soon be extinct because there are not enough of them to recover, no matter what we do. Many animals, particularly smaller ones such as insects and sponges, are becoming extinct before we have even studied them.

Dodo
The slow and clumsy, flightless dodo birds lived on Mauritius and Reunion Islands in the Indian Ocean. They became extinct in the 18th century as they were easy prey for hunters.

Dinosaurs

Around 200 million years ago dinosaurs appeared on Earth. They roamed the planet for 140 million years and then suddenly died out. Many scientists believe that a giant meteor crashed into the sea and caused a change in the climate that killed off the dinosaurs.

Extinct animals

Extinct means that the last living individual of a species has died or been killed, and that species has vanished from the Earth forever. Extinctions are gathering pace and in the 1990s at least one species probably disappears every day. Still more species are on the slippery slope toward extinction unless we change what we are doing to animals, their habitats, and the planet on which we all live. Some extinct animals are:

- Dodo 1770
- Bali Tiger 1937
- Passenger Pigeon 1914
- Texas Red Wolf 1970
- Huia 1907
- Kamchutka Bear 1920
- Florida Black Wolf 1917
- Cape Verde Giant Skink 1940
- Arizona Jaguar 1905
- Round Island Boa 1980
- Mexican Silver Grizzly Bear 1967
- Tasmanian Wolf 1933
- Leopard Frog 1930s
- Lake Titicaca Orestras 1950s

Huia

The huia birds lived in the forests of New Zealand's North Island. People hunted them and destroyed their forest habitat. By 1907 the species had been killed off.

We know about dinosaurs and other extinct animals by examining their fossilized bones.

Mexican silver grizzly bear

Known as "the silver one," this bear was hunted until there were no more alive. In 1960 there were only 30 left in the world, but still the ranchers killed them, until by 1967 they had all disappeared.

Lake Titicaca orestra

Orestras were unique fish that lived only in LakeTiticaca, U.S., because they preferred shallow water and never left the lake to explore the rivers. In 1937, the U.S. government put lake trout into the water. The trout ate many of the smaller creatures in the lake, including the young orestras. By 1950 there were no more orestras left.

Passenger pigeon

At one time, passenger pigeons covered much of eastern North America, living in the trees across the land. Out of every ten birds in North America, four were passenger pigeons. They were once the most numerous birds in existence. Between 1860 and 1900, humans hunted and killed all of them except one—Martha. Martha spent the last 14 years of her life in Cincinnati Zoo, U.S., where she died in 1914.

Florida black wolf

From Florida to Georgia, Alabama and Tennessee, the black wolf roamed the swamps, forests, plains, and hills of the U.S. in great numbers. Then in the 1800s humans began to settle on the land, chopping down trees, building houses, farming the land and eating the wildlife. Huge numbers of black wolves starved to death. Those that were left were shot, trapped, or poisoned. By 1917 there were no more black wolves.

Endangered animals

AN ANIMAL SPECIES IS ENDANGERED when the number of individuals alive falls so low, they may not be able to bear enough young to continue their species. Species become endangered for many reasons. Sometimes animals are killed by humans. Animals also die because their habitats are destroyed and they lose their homes or food supplies. Today, 1,096 species are at risk of extinction and 169 are very, very close.

Gorillas

Gorillas are killed for different parts of their bodies, which are used in medicines or sold as souvenirs to tourists. Sometimes young gorillas are sold to zoos. Often their home forests are cleared for the wood or the land for farming.

Bears

Bears are endangered because of the way that humans treat them. They are caught and kept in cages too small for them, and their bile is tapped for Chinese medicine. Others are used as dancing or fighting bears for the tourist trade.

Manatee

The gentle, large-eyed manatees live and swim in the coastal seas and waterways where humans also play and hunt. Many of their deaths are human-related. The manatee, who cradles her young in her arms, is probably the mermaid we read of in myths and legends.

Conservation

Conservation is a way of preserving the planet and its life forms by setting aside areas of land on which the plants that grow and the animals that live are protected. Only a very small percentage of the world's land surface and its wild spaces are protected in this way. Agreements between countries, such as CITES (Convention on International Trade in Endangered Species) also help to protect animals.

Zoos

Zoos are places where wild animals are kept in captivity, often species of which there are only a few left, so that they can breed in safety. Some zoos run education programs to teach people how to protect species.

Reserves

Reserves are areas of land or water where wild animals are protected from being hunted and can live and breed in safety. The world's first reserve was the Yellowstone National Park in the U.S.

Black rhino

The black rhino is an African rhino, killed mainly for its horn. The horn is powdered and used in oriental medicines, or carved into dagger handles in the Middle East. Rhino horn trade has been banned worldwide for over 20 years, but illegal trade continues. Rhino numbers have dropped 95 percent since 1970.

Things you can do to help

Every small thing we can each do to help preserve the Earth's animal species will help turn the tide of their existence away from extinction toward continued life. You can:

1) Join one of the organizations listed at the back of this book.
2) Refuse to buy products that contain animal ingredients, such as fur, ivory, and tortoise shell.
3) Refuse to buy products that have been tested on animals.
4) Think about what you eat.
5) Start or join a local community effort to save an area of land used by wildlife.
6) Buy recycled paper and save paper for recycling to help conserve forested habitats.
7) Make a mini-wildlife reserve in your back garden or at your school.
8) Refuse to buy pets, such as parrots, that have been caught in the wild and transported to your country.
9) Learn as much as you can about how animals become endangered and find out more ways in which to help them.

Glossary

ACCELERATE To increase the speed of motion

ALIEN A being or thing foreign to its environment

ALTITUDE The vertical height of an object

AMNESIA A defect in memory

ANCIENT EGYPT The time when Egypt was ruled by the pharaohs between 3100 B.C. and 30 B.C.

ANCIENT GREECE The time when the Greeks set up a society that became the most influential in the world from 1500 B.C. to 323 B.C.

ANCIENT ROME The time when the Roman Empire ruled western Europe, the Middle East, and the north coast of Africa from 753 B.C. to A.D. 476

ANTARCTIC The continent around the South Pole and the surrounding waters where average temperatures are all below freezing

ANTENNAE A pair of mobile feelers on the heads of insects, crustaceans etc. that often respond to touch and taste

AQUATIC Living, growing, or found in water

BACTERIA A large group of microorganisms many of which cause disease

BEAST OF BURDEN An animal such as a horse, donkey, or ox used for carrying loads

BILL The projecting jaws of a bird covered with a horny sheath

BIOSPHERE The part of the Earth's surface and atmosphere inhabited by living things

BIRD Any warm-blooded egg-laying vertebrate characterized by a body covering of feathers and wings

BREED To produce or cause to produce by mating

CAMOUFLAGE The means by which animals escape the notice of predators

CAPTIVITY Imprisonment

CARCASE The dead body of an animal

CARNIVORE Any animal or plant that feeds on animals

CHRISTIAN Relating to or derived from Jesus Christ, his teachings, example, or followers

CHRYSALIS The pupa of a moth or butterfly, in a case or cocoon

CLASSICAL Relating to or characteristic of the ancient Greeks and Romans or their civilization

CLIMATE The long-term weather conditions of an area

COCOON A silky protective envelope secreted by silkworms and certain insect larvae in which the pupae develop

COLONY A group of the same type of animal or plant living or growing together

COMMUNITY A group of interdependent plants and animals inhabiting the same region

COMPOUND EYE The eye of some insects and some crustaceans consisting of numerous separate light-sensitive units

CONSERVATION The act of protecting, preserving, and careful management of natural resources

CONSTELLATION Any of the groups of stars as seen from Earth many of which were named by the ancient Greeks after animals or mythological persons

CORRAL An enclosure for cattle or horses

CREVASSE A break in a river embankment

CRUSTACEAN Any invertebrate having jointed limbs, a segmented body, and an outer-skeleton made of chitin of the aquatic class, such as crabs and lobsters

CUB The young of certain animals such as foxes, wolves, lions, and bears

CUD Partially digested food regurgitated from the first stomach to the mouth to be chewed again

CULTIVATE To plant, tend, harvest or improve

CULTURE The total of the inherited ideas, beliefs, values, and knowledge of a society or a particular civilization at a particular period

DESCENDANT Something that derives from an earlier form

DISCIPLE A follower a teacher or a school of thought

DOMESTIC Bred or kept by humans as a pet or for purposes such as the supply of food

DOMINANT Having primary authority or influence

ECHOLOCATION Determination of the position of an object by bouncing sound off it and measuring the time it takes

ELONGATED Extra-long or extended

EMBLEM A badge or pictorial symbol

EMPATHY A deep understanding for another person's or animal's feelings

ENDANGERED In danger of extinction

ENVIRONMENT The surroundings in which an animal lives that influence its development and behavior

EQUALITY The state of being equal

ESTIMATE To calculate roughly

EVOLUTION The gradual change in the characteristics of a population of animals or plants over successive generations

EXTINCT Having died out

FIELD OF VISION The area that the eye is able to see without having to turn the head

FLOCK A group of animals of one kind especially sheep or birds

FOOD CHAIN A series of organisms in a community each of which feeds on another in the chain and is in turn eaten

FOSSIL A relic of a plant or animal that existed in a past age in the form of mineralized bones, shells etc.

FRESHWATER Of or living in fresh water

GENETICS The study of heredity and variation in organisms

GLOBAL WARMING An increase in the average temperature worldwide believed to be caused by the greenhouse effect

GRAZE To feed on the vegetation on a patch of land

GREENHOUSE EFFECT The warming up of the Earth due to human-made carbon dioxide in the atmosphere that traps the infrared radiation emitted by the Earth's surface

HABITAT The natural home of an animal

HARNESS The arrangement of straps fitted to an animal so that the animal can pull a cart

HERBIVORE An animal that feeds on grass and other plants

HERD A large group of mammals living and feeding together

HIBERNATE To pass the winter in a dormant condition

HINDU Relating to the complex beliefs and customs which are the dominant religion of India

HIVE A natural or artificial structure for housing a colony of bees

HYPOTHERMIA An abnormally low body temperature caused by exposure to cold

IMMATURE Not fully grown or developed

IMMORTAL Not subject to death or decay

IMMUNE Protected from infection or danger

INCUBATE To supply eggs with heat to help them hatch

INSTINCT The behavioral reactions that an animal is born with and does not have to learn

INVERTEBRATE Any animal lacking a backbone

JEWISH Characteristic of the religion of the Jews, based on the Old Testament and having as its central point a belief in one God

KIN A class or group with similar characteristics

LARVAE Young of many animals that develop into a different adult form by metamorphosis

LATIUM An ancient territory in Italy inhabited by Latin people from 10 B.C.–4 B.C.

LEGEND A popular story passed on from earlier times whose truth has not been confirmed

LIFE CYCLE The series of changes in the life of an animal between one stage and the identical stage in the next generation

LOTUS A water plant with large leaves, a beautiful perfume and pinkish flowers, regarded as sacred in ancient Egypt

MAMMAL Any of a large class of warm-blooded vertebrates which feeds milk to its young

MEMBRANE A thin layer of tissue that covers or connects inner parts of an animal's body

MIDDLE AGES The period from about 1000 A.D. to the 15th century

MIGRATE To journey between specific habitats at specific times of the year

MIMIC To imitate or copy

MUSLIM Relating to the doctrines and culture of Islam

MUZZLE The projecting part of the head, usually the jaws and nose of animals such as the horse and dog

MYTH A story about superhuman beings of an earlier age

MYXOMATOSIS A highly infectious, usually fatal disease of rabbits

NATIVE Born in a specified place

NATIVE AMERICAN A person who belongs to the race of people who were the original inhabitants of America, as distinguished from invaders or settlers

NAVIGATE To direct oneself carefully or safely

NOCTURNAL Being active at night

NORSE Characteristic of Norway

OPPORTUNIST A person or animal that seizes opportunities when available

OPPOSABLE THUMB A thumb that can be placed opposite the other digits (fingers) so as to be able to touch the ends of each

ORAL Spoken as opposed to written form of communication

ORPHANAGE A home for the care and protection of abandoned children

PACK A group of animals of the same kind

PACKHORSE Horse used to transport goods and equipment for humans

PAGAN Without religion

PARADOX A person or thing exhibiting apparently contradictory characteristics

PARASITE An animal that lives off another

PERSECUTE To oppress, harass, or maltreat

POLLINATE To transfer the substance produced by one part of a seed-bearing plant to another to allow it to reproduce

POLLUTION Poisonous or harmful substances

POPULATIONS A group of individuals of the same species inhabiting a given area

POROUS Lets in water, air, or other fluids

PREDATOR Any carnivorous animal

PREDICT To make known in advance

PREHISTORIC Relating to human development before the written word

PREVAIL To prove superior

PRIDE A group of lions

PRIMATE A mammal having flexible hands, good eyesight, and a highly developed brain including apes and humans

PROSPERITY The condition of prospering

PROVOKE To anger

PTERODACTYL An extinct flying reptile

PUPA The inactive non-feeding stage of development of some insects between the larvl and adult stages when many internal changes occur

PUPATE To develop into a pupa

PURIFY To make clean

RARE Not widely distributed

RECYCLE To reclaim or pass through a system for further use

REGURGITATE To bring back into the mouth after swallowing

REPTILE Any of the cold-blooded vertebrates characterized by lungs, an outer covering of horny scale or plates, and young produced in eggs such as tortoises, snakes, lizards, and crocodiles

RUDDER Anything that guides or directs

RUMP The hindquarters of an animal, not including the legs

SCAVENGER Any animal that feeds on decaying matter

SCENT A smell left by an animal

SECRETION A substance released from a plant or animal cell

SENSES The faculties by which the mind of an animal receives information about the external world

SHED To cast off or lose

SIGN LANGUAGE The visual communication of coded symbols made with the hands

SOLITARY Not living in organized colonies or large groups

SPECIES A group of animals that are capable of interbreeding and that share common attributes

SPIRIT Vital force that animates the body of living beings

STABILIZER Any device that makes something steady

STEALTHY Secretive, unobserved

SUBCONSCIOUS The part of the mind on the edge of consciousness

SUPERSTITION Irrational belief especially with regard to the unknown

SURPLUS A quantity or amount extra to what is needed

SYMBOL Something that represents or stands for something else

TALON A sharply-hooked claw

TAME Changed by humans from a wild state into a domesticated condition

TECHNOLOGY The practical use of science and knowledge

TERRITORY An area inhabited and defended by an animal or pair of animals

TICKS Blood-sucking parasites

TIGRESS A female tiger

TRANCE A slightly dazed state resembling sleep

VARIETY A race whose distinct characteristics do not justify classification as a separate species

VEGETATION Plant life as a whole

VENOM A poisonous fluid secreted by animals such as snakes

VERTEBRATES Any animal characterized by a bony skeleton and a well-developed brain including fishes, amphibians, reptiles, birds, and mammals

VULNERABLE Capable of being damaged or destroyed

WARM-BLOODED Having a constant body temperature usually higher than the surrounding environment

WATERFOWL Any aquatic freshwater bird

WILD Not domesticated or tame

WILDLIFE RESERVE A protected area of land or water where animals can live in as natural a state as possible

WORSHIP To be devoted to and full of admiration for

WRATH Angry indignation

Zoo Place where living animals are kept, studied, bred, and exhibited to the public

Index

Aa

Bb

Cc

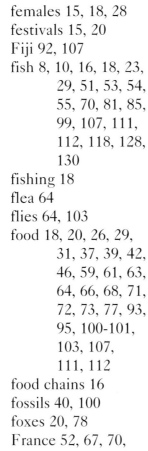

Useful addresses

When writing to these societies please remember to enclose a stamped, addressed envelope. Many of these groups have a junior club or newsletter and will send you lots of useful information.

COMPASSION IN WORLD FARMING
20, Lavant St
Petersfield
Hampshire
GU32 3EW
UK
Tel: +44 0730 264208
Fax: +44 0730 260791

ROYAL SOCIETY FOR THE
PROTECTION OF BIRDS
The Lodge
Sandy
Bedfordshire
SE1 2DL
UK
Tel: +44 01767 680551

MARINE CONSERVATION SOCIETY LTD
9, Gloucester Rd
Ross-on-Wye
Herefordshire
HR9 5BU
UK
Tel: +44 0989 66017
Fax: +44 0989 67815

WORLD SOCIETY FOR THE
PROTECTION OF ANIMALS
2, Langley Lane
London
SW8 1TJ
UK
Tel: +44 0171 793 0540

INTERNATIONAL DOLPHIN WATCH
Parklands
North Ferriby
Humberside
HU14 3ET
UK
Tel: +44 0482 634350

ANIMAL AID
The Old Chapel
Bradford St
Tonbridge
Kent
TN9 1AW
UK
Tel: +44 0732 364546
Fax: +44 0732 366533

ANIMALS' DEFENDERS
261-263 Goldhawk Rd
London
W12 9PE
UK
Tel: +44 0181 846 9777
Fax: +44 0181 846 9712

BRITISH HEDGEHOG PRESERVATION SOCIETY
Knowbury House
Knowbury
Ludlow
Shropshire
SY8 3LQ
UK
Tel: +44 0584 890287

LEAGUE AGAINST CRUEL SPORTS LTD
83/87 Union St
London
SE1 1SG
UK
Tel: +44 0171 403 6155

WHALE AND DOLPHIN CONSERVATION SOCIETY
20, West Lea Rd
Bath
Avon
BA1 3RL
UK
Tel: +44 0225 334511
Fax: +44 0225 480097

YOUNG PEOPLE'S TRUST FOR ENDANGERED
SPECIES
19, Quarry Street
Guildford
Surrey
GU1 3EH
UK
Tel: +44 0483 39600
Fax: +44 0483 301996

ELEFRIENDS
Cherry Tree Cottage
Coldharbour
Near Dorking
Surrey
RH5 6HA
UK
Tel: +44 081 682 1818

WATCH TRUST FOR ENVIRONMENTAL
EDUCATION
22, The Green
Nettleham
Lincoln
LN2 2NR
UK
Tel: + 44 0522 544400
Fax: +44 0522 511616

THE VEGETARIAN SOCIETY
Parkdale
Dunham Rd
Altrincham
Cheshire
WA14 4QC
UK
Tel: +44 061 928 0793
Fax: +44 061 926 9182

WILDFOWL AND WETLANDS TRUST
SLIMBRIDGE
Gloucester
GL2 7BT
UK
Tel: + 44 01453 890333
Fax: +44 01453 890827

FRIENDS OF THE EARTH INTERNATIONAL
P O Box 19199
1000 GD Amsterdam
The Netherlands
Tel: +010 31 20 622 1369
Fax: +010 31 20 639 2181

GREENPEACE INTERNATIONAL
Keizersgracht 176
1016 DW Amsterdam
The Netherlands
Tel: +010 31 20 523 6555

WILDLIFE AFRICA CONSERVATION
129a Kitson St
Northcliff
Johannesburg
South Africa
Tel: +27 11 7823410

NATURE BASE WESTERN AUSTRALIA
Hackett Drive
Crawley 6009
Australia
Tel: +08 9442 0300
Fax: +08 9386 1578

NATURAL RESOURCES CONSERVATION SERVICE
P O Box 2890
Washington DC 20013
USA

CONSERVATION INTERNATIONAL
2501 M Street, NW
Suite 200
Washington DC 20037
USA
Tel: 202 429 5660
Fax: 202 887 0193

Websites

THE WORLD WILDLIFE FUND FOR NATURE
http://wwf.org

BAT CONSERVATION INTERNATIONAL TOP PAGE
http://www.batcon.org/index.html

EARTH AND SKY HOME PAGE
http://www.earthsky.com

INTERNATIONAL WILDLIFE EDUCATION
& CONSERVATION HOME PAGE
http://www.iwec.org

THE TIGER INFORMATION CENTER
http://www.5tigers.org

THE INTERNATIONAL RHINO FOUNDATION
http://www.rhinos-irf.org/

THE WORLD CONSERVATION MONITORING
CENTRE UK
http://www.wcmc.org.uk

PET CHANNEL USA
http://www.thepetchannel.com/

ELEPHANT SANCTUARY
http://www.elephants.com/mission.htm

THE GORILLA FOUNDATION
http://www.gorilla.org

THE ROOKERY PENGUIN PAGES
http://www.webcom.com/~jmallen/pages.html

SEA SHEPHERD CONSERVATION SOCIETY
http://www.seashepherd.org/

UNIQUE AUSTRALIAN ANIMALS
http://werple.mira.net/~areadman/aussie.htm

IUCN WORLD CONSERVATION UNION—
SLOVAKIA
http://www.fris.uniba.sk/zp/iucn/eng/projekt
y/dec/index.htm

WILDLIFE CONSERVATION
http://rhrwildlife.com/conserve.htm

EUROPEAN CENTRE FOR NATURE
CONSERVANCY http://www.ecnc.nl/

RAINFOREST ACTION NETWORK
http://www.ran.org/

HAWKWATCH INTERNATIONAL
http://www.hawkwatch.org

WILDLIFE AFRICA CONSERVATION
http://www.wildlifeafrica.co.za/conservation.
html

KUAOTUNU KIWI SANCTUARY
http://www.mercury.co.nz/Khs.html

CANADIAN WORLD PARROT TRUST
http://wchat.on.ca/parrot/cwparrot.htm

INTERNATIONAL FUND FOR ANIMAL WELFARE
http://www.ifaw.org

NATURAL RESOURCES
CONSERVATION
SERVICE
http://ww.nrcs.
usda.gov/

CONSERVATION
INTERNATIONAL
http://www.
conservation.org

Acknowledgments

BAMPTON-BETTS would like to thank everyone who helped in the production of this book, especially Janine Amos for editorial assistance, and Marie-Clare Carver at Illustration, Mike Croll from Wildlife Art, Virgil Pomfret Agency, and Bernard Thornton Artists for illustration assistance and Elaine Ackerley at the Natural History Photographic Agency, Vicki Skeet at the Natural History Museum, Clive Smith at the Telegraph Colour Library, and Charlotte Lorimer at the Bridgeman Art Library for picture research and assistance.

Abbreviations: t=top; b=bottom; c=center; l=left; r=right; FC=front cover; BC=back cover; FCF=front cover flap; BCF=back cover flap

Picture credits:
B. & C. Alexander/NHPA 54tr
A.N.T./NHPA 102tl
Anthony Bannister/NHPA 54lc, 71tr, 115tl
Henry Ausloos/NHPA 142bl, 143c
G. I. Bernard/NHPA 54br, 64bl, 92tl, 141tr
Joe Blossom/NHPA 74b
Ian Bradshaw/Telegraph Colour Library 40-41c
Laurie Campbell/NHPA 55tl, 83bl, 116tr
Stephen Dalton/NHPA FCcr, FCtl, FCc, BCcl, 51tr, 58bl, 60bl, 70-71c,
Susanne Danegger/NHPA 37tl
Nigel J. Dennis/NHPA 107c
European Space Agency/Science Photo Library 8tl
E Hanumantha Rao/NHPA 17t
Martin Harvey/NHPA 115br, 142b
Daniel Heuclin/NHPA 52bl, 89tc, 114tr
E.A. Janes/NHPA 77t
B Jones and M Shimlock/NHPA 55bl, 84c, 93br
Rich Kirchner/NHPA 14b, 69bl
Stephen Krafemann/NHPA 12c
Gerard Lacz/NHPA 22-23, 115tr
Jay Pack Picture Library/Telegraph Colour Library 129tr
Haroldo Palo Jr/NHPA 8b, 8tr
Louvre, Paris/The Bridgeman Art Library 52tr
NASA 41tr
Eero Murtomaki/NHPA 56c
David E Myers/NHPA 71c
National Gallery, London/Bridgeman Art Library 124 tl
Pinacoteca Capitolina, Palazzo Conservatori, Rome/The Bridgeman Art Library 29tr
Haroldo Palo Jr/NHPA 73c
Peter Pickford FCtr, BCbr
Rod Planck/NHPA 44l
Christophe Ratier/NHPA 139r
Andy Rouse/NHPA 24-25t

John Sanford and David Parker/Science Photo Library 118tr
Jany Sauvanet/NHPA 70bl, 114lc
Kevin Schafer/NHPA 49tl, 50bl, 106b
John Shaw/NHPA FCc, 19, 54bl, 55br, 120c
Science Photo Library FCc
Stephen Simpson/Telegraph Colour Library 35tc
Eric Soder/NHPA 55tr, 113tr
H Sykes/Telegraph Colour Library 125b
The Natural History Museum, London FCcl
Michael Tweedie/NHPA 63br
Hellio & Van Ingen/NHPA 91t
Martin Wendler/NHPA 90-91b
Peter Willi/Bridgeman Art Library 34bl
Bill Wood/NHPA 98tl
David Woodfall/NHPA 55rc, 68bl
Norbert Wu/NHPA 88tl, 114bl

Illustrations by:
Adam Abel 62-63c, 91br, 92-93bl, 125cr, 148tl
Craig Austin 48-49bl-c, 86-87b, 88-89c
Alan Baker 47tr, 124-125c, 130-131c
John Barber 66-67c, 108c
Andy Beckett 17b, 36bl, 154tl
Lesley Betts 18t, 45tr
Lucy Bristow 80-81c
Wayne Ford 3c, 30b, 38b, 44-45c
Lena Fricher 34-35c
Roger Gorringe 58-59c, 100-101c
Darren Harvey 98-99c
Tim Hayward 50c, 142br
Martin Knowlden BCFb, 46bl, 127tr, 132b, 134-135c, 145br, 159c
Josephine Martin 75tr, 104-105c
Danuta Mayer FCFb, 32bl, 74tl, 135tr
Steve Noon 1c, 15b, 20-21c, 28-29c, 32-33c, 78l, 92-93c
Richard Orr 9, 10-11
Steve Roberts 51br, 54-55c, 94-95c, 102-103c, 140-141c, 147bl, 155br
Andrew Robinson 4b, 64-65c, 151br
Judy Stephens 40tl, 96tl, 98cl
Mark Stewart 76c, 152bl
Simon Turvey 6t, 112b, 114-115c
Unterliden Museum, Colmar, France 126b
Garry Walton FCtc, BCtc, FCFtc, 1t, 3t, 122-123c, 123tr, 127cr, 128-129c, 136bl, 138-139c
Andrew Wheatcroft 42-43c, 116bl, 136-137c
Nadine Wickenden borders throughout book
Sarah Young 4t, 21tr, 64tl, 109tr, 118c, 119c, 130tl, 134tl, 136tl

Dover Books for all black and white line illustrations
Panda device © 1986 WWF – World Wide Fund for Nature (formerly World Wildlife Fund) 22t

Please note that every effort has been made to trace copyright holders. Element Children's Books apologizes in advance for any unintentional omissions and would be glad to include an appropriate acknowledgment in subsequent editions of this publication.